Starting Up!

Insights for startups and small business –

From a master entrepreneur

New, expanded second edition

Dave Berkus

Published by David Berkus.

For corrections, company/title updates, comments, or any other inquiries, please e-mail DBerkus@berkus.com

Second Printing 2014
10 9 8 7 6 5 4 3 2

ISBN 978-1-105-03945-4

The content within this book has been previously published within the books, BASIC BERKONOMICS, BERKONOMICS, and ADVANCED BERKONOMICS. Individual insights from this book are published periodically in Dave's emails and blog, www.berkonomics.com.

Groups may order copies of the book at a group discount by contacting Dave Berkus at 626-355-5375, or at dberkus@berkus.com .

Throughout this book, the Cambria type font was used for headlines, and text was set using the Calibri font.

The views expressed by the individuals in this book do not necessarily reflect the views shared by the companies they are employed by (or the companies mentioned in) this book. The employment status and affiliations of author with the companies referenced are subject to change.

INTRODUCTION

This book is the first in a series of eight short, easy to read books that guide an entrepreneur through the stages of creation, management, growth, and ultimately sale of a small business enterprise. And this is the second edition of this book, packed with half again as much materials the first edition, published in 2011.

Each section is an insight into another facet of starting a business that is not taught in business school or available in business texts, but rather the result of over fifty years of entrepreneurial experience with my own entrepreneurial companies and serving as investor, coach, mentor and board member for over forty entrepreneurial startups over the years.

Originally published as portions of three books, BASIC BERKONOMICS, BERKONOMCS, and ADVANCED BERKONOMICS, comments from entrepreneurs and professional managers after reading those books led to suggestions that I create separate mini-books for each stage of the business, to appeal to the interests of those at that stage of development, ready to absorb and implement insights that apply directly to the current stage of their business. Make them inexpensive and available as eBooks, they suggested, so that entire teams of managers could use the book as a planning tool and discussion prompt for the team in meetings.

And so this series of Small Business Success Books was born to address an opportunity. You can pick up this book and immediately relate to the insights, issues, opportunities, and exercises in this book right at the earliest stages of creating your business. This is not a replacement for "how to" books, courses, and consultants. It is a deeper opportunity to evaluate, plan, and execute strategies for growth based upon these insights that augment and amplify the usual "how to" materials available to entrepreneurs.

In this book, I'll tell personal stories from my fifty-plus years of entrepreneurial experience. But every one of us has a story to add to this mix, one of passionate entrepreneurism, sometimes inside an existing larger corporation, sometimes alone on a kitchen table, or back room desk. And it is a sure thing that many of us will have cogent, insightful additions to this caldron, culled from their own experiences. There's a place for these in the blog, www.berkonomics.com, and I welcome any and all for others to read and learn.

Dave Berkus

Arcadia, California

P.S. This is the sixteenth publication from *The Berkus Press*. I am very fortunate to have expert help this time from some very smart friends in the business, each of whom has volunteered to contribute one or more insights for this book, directly from their personal experience of working as an entrepreneur or with entrepreneurs.   Here's a special thanks to these friends, whose contributions are definitely for your benefit. Whenever one of these excellent insights appear in this book, the first time each contributor's work appears, I'll insert a very short bio for that expert right below the headline. And as always, if no attribution appears for an insight, I'm its author - and to be blamed for any and all errors in judgment and accuracy.

Contents

Starting Up!

Find your rock in Ensenada.

Every entrepreneur has that moment of truth – the one that marks the decision to take the path to entrepreneurship or the path to job security with a larger employer. And down the road a bit, most of us face another when deciding whether or not to go for growth, requiring new investment and increased risks.

My moment of self-confrontation came many years ago when deciding whether to leave behind the relative comfort of a good income from my one person operation or hire my first employee which would allow me to spend my time in sales and in growing the business. It was perhaps the most difficult decision of my young life. Just out of college, managing a business that had paid my way through college and several years beyond, the cost of expansion would cut my take-home income enough to impact my life style and perhaps, if not quickly successful, cause me to put off my pending marriage.

Not a small decision. So I got in my car with a small overnight bag, pointed toward Mexico, and headed to Ensenada, a place I had been to a number of times before, to find solitude for a short weekend just to think about the future.

Checking into an inn I had visited before, which was located right on the beach, I walked out to the shore and found a large, smooth rock, perfect for a long, hopefully productive sit. And I sat. I sat for five hours that night, thinking about the alternatives and what I really wanted for myself over time.

After that evening of isolated, quiet thought, it was clear to me that I wanted to take the risks, to go for it, to attempt to build a big business, to leave my comfort zone.

The next morning, I returned to the rock and sat. Planning 'how,' now that I was comfortable with the 'what and when.' And after a few more hours, I had devised my personal plan. I would hire one full time employee and one independent contractor for a start. I'd take no bank loans or ask for any outside investment. This would be entirely my risk to take unaided. Satisfied, I left that rock, checked out of the seaside inn, and drove home excited and ready to execute my plan.

The story is true. The outcome was excellent. I grew that company to over fifty employees, even taking it public after a number of years, and later selling my interest in that first company to get into the computer software business, just at the right time to take advantage of its amazingly rapid growth.

But it all started with the decision on that rock. If you have a life-changing decision to make – including whether to start your entrepreneurial journey – have you identified *your* rock in Ensenada? Do you have a quiet place where cell phone, text and other distractions can't reach you while you dig deeply into a problem or opportunity?

As we start this book and its description of your journey to entrepreneurial success, I challenge you to find your own special rock in Ensenada – your special quiet place.

The thrill of the adventure!

There is nothing quite as thrilling in business as igniting a startup and watching it blossom. Especially when starting a company with personal savings or money from relatives and friends, early signs of success are intoxicating. Each new customer, each mention in the press or online adds to the feeling of early accomplishment. And it is more satisfying because it is yours, from idea to execution.

But the excitement begins much earlier. With newfound freedom to make independent decisions about finding a company name, where to locate the company, whether to lease an office or start from home, how to engage talent, even whether to provide free coffee to employees, the newly minted entrepreneur can only think of positive thoughts and great outcomes.

This moment is not to be spoiled by such mundane warnings from advisors or consultants to plan carefully, research the market and competition, and execute the plan with tenacity and enthusiasm. This moment is to be enjoyed for what it is: the ignition point in which the dream becomes a reality and anything is possible.

This moment is to celebrate every action, including shopping for supplies, furniture and technology to support the newly minted enterprise. There is never again going to be such a pristine, simple, problem-free time in the life of this business. Relish the experience of creation. Celebrate each important "first," including the first customer order, the first day in a new office, the first new employee hired, the first earned dollar actually deposited into the bank account.

Because it is yours to write alone, there is no Hollywood script more thrilling than the one you create during those first days when everything is so very new.

Be flexible. Be coachable.

As an early stage investor, the first test for me is whether the entrepreneur is flexible in both the plan and execution of his or her vision (since from experience almost everything about a business plan changes over time), and whether the entrepreneur, no matter what age or experience, is coachable.

Doctoral theses have been written on this subject. Early stage investor groups often list these traits at or near the top of their list when filtering opportunities for investment. And I have numerous stories from personal experience that reinforce these two traits as the most positive indicators of future success in business.

In my book, *"Extending the Runway"* (Aspatore Press, 2006), I explore the thesis that there are five basic types of resources an entrepreneur must exploit in growing a successful business: **time, money, process, relationships and context**. Understanding the effects of each upon an entrepreneur and early stage business plan is critical. Being able to adapt to the realities and changes in the fast-moving environment is essential.

Flexibility: the context in which a business plan envisions the enterprise in its marketplace is constantly changing as new products and services challenge competitors to innovate and adapt. A plan written last month may easily need tweaking this month to recognize changes in the marketplace, the central context of the plan itself. Everything happens faster these days than even a few years ago, especially in the arena of technology, where many new businesses are developed each month to solve problems or take advantage of opportunities that existed at the moment of an entrepreneur's vision for the future.

And the money and time required to bring the young company from idea to market extends out as changes require rethinking the plan.

We'll explore this reality in later insights as we explore the stages of business development.

One of the best indicators of future success for an entrepreneur and an early stage idea is the quality and depth of great relationships with industry veterans or technology gurus, or experienced successful business leaders. Those relationships would be impressive but worthless if the entrepreneur was not coachable, open to suggestion and criticism from those who have experience enough to surface the issues unspoken but obvious to the coach.

And finally, there are always ways to improve the process of design, test, roll-out and marketing a new idea. And many potential coaches out there have made mistakes in these processes at the expense of their employers or even their personal savings. Since we all learn from our mistakes, it seems reasonable that we should learn from the mistakes of others, particularly those who freely offer their experiences as lessons for our enterprise.

I've seen entrepreneurs go through the complete process of raising money for a business from investors, many of whom were experienced and well beyond just friends and family, only to ignore all advice and execute a flawed business plan to death, ignoring the pleas and attempts at coaching by others including those investors.

Don't be one of those. Be flexible and be coachable.

Do you have that entrepreneurial DNA?

My immediate family members were entrepreneurs from as far back as I can trace. Dad was a jeweler, then a furniture store owner. Mom wrote books and articles from her college days until she could no longer see the keyboard. One grandfather owned and maintained his apartment houses. The other was a grocer, then a jeweler.

So it seemed perfectly natural that my brother and I find our separate callings as entrepreneurs from the very start. I took pictures of neighbor children, developing them in my bedroom closet, selling the prints to those neighborhood families. I was twelve. The prints were not very good. At fifteen, I started a recording business that would pay my way through college, a business that I'd take public in a limited IPO years after, before getting into the computer software business in its infancy. My brother, who had an artist streak where no-one could identify its roots, drew pictures that were extraordinary, and became one of the world's one hundred most noted architects.

What drove my brother and me to perform, to risk so much, to skirt bankruptcy, to press on again and again? For us, I believe it was two important things. First, our family DNA made us comfortable talking about risk and self-discovery in running a business, even without formal training. Second, and more importantly, my brother and I watched our dad run his business in the most conservative manner possible, refusing to expand or take risks, comfortable with a steady income and no prospects of building wealth through building business equity. Both of us reacted in different ways, but in common was the urge to take much more risk, to push the boundaries, to succeed spectacularly or fail and start again. We reacted to our view of dad's conservatism.

We tell the story that dad was offered the general store franchise in the brand new park in Anaheim soon to be built by Walt Disney. The price for the franchise in 1953 was $50,000. Dad turned it down, stating that there was no chance of success for a park so far from downtown Los

Angeles. His two sons observed, and perhaps reacted in later years by pushing to take the chance for themselves equal to that declined by dad.

Are you a DNA-based entrepreneur? Or are you starting out to build the next Cisco Systems because you know how your employer has failed to do so? Or do you want freedom from the senseless bureaucracy you face daily in your present job? Have you found the cure for cancer and need to bring it to the world? Or is your reason for risk more basic – that you found an easy opportunity to fill a need and you have the skill and desire to take that chance.

Think for a minute about your real reasons for taking this ride. It will help you to make better decisions about future risk, about your tolerance for it, and about your inner-self.

The most important person on the startup team
By David S. Rose

David S. Rose: Described by BusinessWeek as a "world conquering entrepreneur" and by Forbes as "New York's Archangel", David is a former Inc. 500 CEO, serial entrepreneur and the founder of New York Angels. He is the founder and CEO of Gust, the angel financing platform used by over 50,000 accredited investors in 1,000 angel groups and venture capital funds to collaborate with over 250,000 entrepreneurs in 95 countries.

Since Bill Hewlett joined with Dave Packard in 1939 to create what is today one of the world's largest computer companies, there has been an evergreen debate as to who is more important in starting a tech company: the techie or the business guy? Steve Jobs or Steve Wozniak? Bill Gates or Steve Ballmer? Jim Clark or Marc Andreessen?

I propose that it is time to reject the notion of the *business man* or *business woman* entirely. The underlying problem is that there are really three different components here, and like the classic three-legged school, they are all essential for success, albeit with differing relative economic values. What confuses us is that the components can all reside in one person, or multiple people. And what upsets people is that there are different quantities of those components available in the economic marketplace; and the law of supply and demand is pretty good about consequently assigning a value to them.

Perhaps surprisingly, the components are NOT the traditional coding/business pieces; nor are they even coding / user interface / business / sales, or whatever. Rather, here is the way I see it, from the perspective of a serial entrepreneur turned serial investor, listed in order of decreasing availability:

1) THE CONCEPT: A business starts with an idea, and while the idea may (and likely will) change over time; it has to be good at some basic level for it to be able to succeed in the long run. How excited am I likely to be when I see a plan for a new generation of buggy whip, or another me-too social network? The basic concept has to make some kind of sense given the technical, market and competitive environment, otherwise nothing else matters. BUT good ideas are NOT hard to find. There are millions of them out there. The key to making one of them into a home-run success brings us to:

2) EXECUTION SKILLS: It is into this one bucket that ALL of the 'traditional' pieces fall. This is where you find the superb Rails coder, *and* the world-class information architect, *and* the consummate sales guy, *and* the persuasive business development person, *and* the brilliant CFO. Each of the functions is crucial, and each is required to bring the good idea to fruition. In our fluid, capitalistic, free-market society, the marketplace is generally very efficient about assigning relative economic value to each of these functional roles, based upon both the direct result of their contribution to the enterprise and their scarcity (or lack thereof) in the job market.

That is why it is not uncommon to see big enterprise sales people making high six figure - or even seven figure - salaries or commissions, while a neophyte coder might be in the low five figure range. Similarly, a crackerjack CTO might be in the mid six figures, but a kid performing inside sales may start at the opposite end of the spectrum. Coding, design, production, sales, finance, operations, marketing, and the like are all execution skills; and without great execution, success will be very hard to come by.

But, as noted, each of these skills is available at a price, and given enough money it is clearly possible to assemble an all-star team in each of the above areas to execute any good idea. That, however, will not be enough. Why? Because it is missing the last, vital leg of the stool, and the one that ultimately–when success does come–will reap the lion's share of the benefits:

3) THE ENTREPRENEUR: Entrepreneurship is at the core of starting a company, whether tech-based or otherwise. It is *not* any one of the functional skills above, but rather the combination of vision, passion, leadership, commitment, communication skills, hypomania, fundability, and, above all, willingness to take risks, that brings together all of the forgoing pieces - and creates from them an enterprise that fills a value-producing role in our economy. And because it is *this* function which is the scarcest of all, it is *this* function that (adjusting for the cost of capital) ends up with the lion's share of the money from a successful venture.

It is crucial to note that the entrepreneurial function can be combined into the same package as a techie (Bill Gates), a sales guy (Mark Cuban), a user interface maven (Steve Jobs), or a financial guy (Michael Bloomberg). And that it is the critical piece which ultimately (if things work out) gets the big bucks.

The moral of the story is that, for a successful company, we need to bring together all of the above pieces, realize that whatever functional skill set the entrepreneur starts out with can be augmented with the others, and understand that the lion's share of the rewards will (after adjusting for the cost of capital), go to the entrepreneurial role, as has happened for hundreds of years.

Plans? Humbug! Show me what you're made of.
By David Steakley

David Steakley, a past President of the Houston Angel Network, is a reformed management consultant. He is an active angel investor, and he manages several angel funds in Texas.

Business plans are interesting. But, as a famous field marshal (1) said, no battle plan survives contact with the enemy. I have found it more important to assess the capabilities of the founding team to react, revise and pivot *(quickly change direction),* than it is important to assess the business plan. How do you know whether your founder team and your added executives have the right stuff to survive contact with the enemy?

In addition to the ability to pivot, character matters, too. As my kids have commenced driving, I've harped incessantly, hopefully to the point of their nausea, on the notion that they should always have in mind that everyone driving on the road is in a massive conspiracy to collide with them, and make it appear that the collision was an accident. "Just assume everyone is trying to kill you," I say.

I take this approach to angel investing. I begin by assuming that the founders of the company are incompetent, psychopathic, lying con-men and thieves; and I try to convict them of these charges. I ask them innocuous questions, and try to check as many seemingly inconsequential details of their story as I can. Where did you go to school? When did you graduate? In what field was your degree? What was your first job? Why did you leave that job? Where did you grow up? Did you play sports in high school? What are your hobbies?

Faithful in little; faithful in much. If someone will deceive about a small matter, he will deceive about anything and everything. I don't do business with liars. If I am unsuccessful in proving these charges, then, perhaps the company is a candidate for investment.

I was a partner at a large global consulting firm. We hired literally hundreds of thousands of graduates every year. They had no meaningful experience. The only way to evaluate them was to look for a kind of raw, athletic talent. To help us in this, we adopted a technique which I believe is now universally used, but which was unusual at the time. We called it *behavioral interviewing*. This technique relies on identifying specific traits and characteristics which one wishes to find, either negatively or positively, and then asking the candidate to tell specific true stories about situations in which s/he would have had an opportunity to demonstrate the traits in question. A lot of the value of this technique relies on the interviewer being extremely aggressive with the candidate about the minutest of details within the story offered.

For the founders of companies in which I am considering investing, I have concluded that flexibility, intellectual nimbleness, and a relentless focus on dispassionate examination of factual evidence of results, are some relatively rare traits with which I cannot ignore. "Tell me about a time when you changed your mind about something important," I will ask. "Tell me about a time when what you were doing wasn't working. How did you know it wasn't working? What was the problem? What did you do?" "Tell me about a time when you screwed up big time. What happened? What did you do?" I will ask questions about the tiniest details of their stories. What were you wearing? What time of day was that?

I have actually had people respond along the lines of "I don't recall a time when I screwed up." Or "Sometimes I have been let down by my subordinates and my partners, though." Check, please!

But, a more common problem is that you find out by detailed questioning that the story presented is not really a true specific story, but a theoretical composite story, which reflects theoretical behavior the interviewee assumes you want to hear about. I don't want to work with these people. They are trying to tell me what I want to hear, and they do not want to admit the possibility of fault.

I want to work with people who are pleased to discover mistakes, errors, and opportunities for improvement. I will not work with people who hide mistakes, who ignore errors, and who pretend that everything is wonderful. I want to work with people who face the truth.

One of my very favorite entrepreneurs is the shining example of taking himself to task over errors and missteps, and of a constant vigilant search for how things are going wrong in his businesses. Recently he launched a unit which developed a casual browser-based online game, monetized through micro-transactions for virtual in-game goods. One of the beautiful things about this kind of business is the depth and immediacy of information available about performance and results. So, when something is changed, you find out immediately how the change affects results. This company has been through so many iterations of its model that I have lost track. I love the willingness to experiment, and the perpetual dissatisfaction with how things are going, and the relentless quest for improvement. This guy is going to make me a lot of money, or die trying.

So, focus on the personal traits and characteristics of your team. Things will definitely go wrong. You want to have some idea of how your team will react when that inevitably happens.

(1)   Helmuth Von Moltke the Elder, 1871

Project cash flow - not just profit - during start-up.

Cash is everything to a new business. How many times do we have to say this? The days of being able to trust that there will be an investor or lender on the other end of a call or email whenever needed ended with the 2000 and 2008 bursts of those respective bubbles. It's entirely possible that Amazon could not be created and funded today with its planned seven years until profitability.

Early stage investors who take a chance on new businesses, often now plan their investments around the notion – or hope – that they can fund one or two rounds to lead the business to profitability. There is no longer a guarantee that VCs and later stage investors will be waiting at the run-out point of the angel money to pick up and grow the company.

Business plans that I see often show three to five years of projections, demonstrating profitability at the end of so many months of operation. Most every one of these uses an accrual basis for determining breakeven, never attempting to predict the cash impact of capital investment, slow collection times, large deposits upon leases, and other major items that consume cash.

Worse yet, most show rapid gains in revenues but do not account for the extra cash it takes for working capital to grow the business at the rate projected. If a business takes an average of sixty days to collect cash from the time it invests in the product with costs of inventory or labor, then shipping and billing, then the business will need increased working capital to pay its expenses including payroll while it waits for the cash to come in the door.

Recast your projections using cash, not accrual, as the measure for planning. An accrual statement is nice to produce. It confirms that the business is capable of ultimately throwing off positive cash flow. But only accurate projections of cash by the week or month as appropriate will assure the survival of a business in a rapid growth cycle, or even a startup raising just enough to make it to breakeven.

Big corporations are just slow to act.
By David Steakley

How do you judge a company's prospects, if a corporate business-to-business sale has to be your game? If your company's market is huge corporations, how do you convince investors you can crack the market, and how do you deliver?

To answer this, you have to understand the challenges of getting paperwork signed and checks issued, in a big company. You'll notice I didn't say "the challenges of selling," because this is seldom the crucial challenge. I am assuming that you have an awesome product or service which cleverly solves some tough problem and promises to deliver solid ROI for the buyer.

Just to be up front, as an investor, I am allergic to companies which rely on making potentially huge sales to corporate clients. The corporate B2B sales cycle produces a harshly binary outcome: either the company dies while waiting for a corporate client to sign the paperwork and remit the funds, or else it delivers gigantic outsized sales with relatively little effort.

I routinely see prospective investments which rely by their nature upon selling to corporate customers. I have learned through bitter experience that little can be predicted from analyzing the company's product or service. Of course, you'd think the company has to have a useful, valuable, or somewhat unusual product in order to be successful. But, from a standpoint of efficient analysis of the company's prospects, this is not the place to start.

Big corporations are just slow to act. The time needed for decision increases as a factor of the number of people involved in the decision process. The number of people involved in the decision process varies as a factor of the amount of money involved, the number of places in the company affected by the transaction, and the duration and contractual obligations of the commitment.

I have found that the predictor of success is really extremely simple: tell me the name, phone number, birthdate and favorite brand of scotch of the senior corporate executive who is going to be your first customer, and tell me how much he is going to pay you in the next twelve months. Now, I am not saying you have to sell only to scotch drinkers, but you get my point: the predictor is your intimate knowledge of people you already know who need your product, want your product, and who know and trust you to the point that they will work hard to overcome the obstacles of closing the deal.

In other words, you have to have inside agents. You have to know, find, create, recruit, whatever, senior corporate executives who will relentlessly and stubbornly perform the unnatural acts required to close the sale.

Occasionally, I have seen success with companies getting started by using channels, i.e., other companies which are already providing or selling some product or service to your customers, who will tuck your product or service into their bag of tricks in return for a slice of the revenue. But it is very, very difficult to get a new product started this way. Once you've established the product, and the channels can be persuaded that your product provides them with relatively easy incremental revenues; channels are a fantastic way to scale your sales effort without fixed costs.

The great advantage of the B2B market is the potentially huge size of revenues from just one sale. Those revenues tend to be very durable, as quite often, you are getting your offerings wired into the DNA of the customer.

Before you tackle the corporate market, be sure you understand the challenges of this market, and think carefully about your product design and your sales approach, to reduce the barriers to closing sales as much as possible.

Plan your exit even as you plan your debut.
By JJ Richa

J.J. Richa is a successful entrepreneur and technologist giving back to the entrepreneurial community in many ways, including his weekly Internet TV program on entrepreneurism, and participation in several mentoring programs.

This insight seems counter-intuitive to many entrepreneurs when starting their fresh, new business.

But when you start a new business, buy an existing business, or as you plan to grow your existing business, one very important aspect to consider is the need to think about your eventual exit. That decision, made at the very start of your effort, determines whether to take outside investor money, "bootstrap" or build it with personal resources only, or some combination.

Are you trying to establish a lifestyle business that generates income without plans to sell it in the future? Or are you building equity in a business that you may want to transform into cash? Depending on your goals, the type of business you choose and the way you grow it should be aligned with your end-game objectives.

Think of potential exit strategies:

- Going Public (IPO)
- Merger (Combine)
- Sale (Acquisition)
- Buyout (LBO, MBO)
- Succession (Family)
- Shutting Down (Asset Liquidation)

Regardless of your situation, it is important to start planning for the end game now. You need to prepare for that exit every step along the way. You'll need to build value and equity in your company by creating unique products, services, relationships and distribution channels, building an intellectual property portfolio and expanding your customer base.

Depending on your situation, an exit may be beneficial to you, your family, your employees, or your investors that helped you get started.

When it comes to your own benefits and the benefit to family and employees - consider all of the time, energy and money you put into your business. It only makes sense to know when and how you will see the rewards of your work. Where do you want to be down the road? How will your business planning and execution help get you there? When do you plan to retire? Without a clear plan to strategically leave your business, you risk never fulfilling both your personal and business goals.

Investors expect to see your ultimate goal to include an exit strategy - at least for them. For the most part, having an exit strategy is one of the ways investors assess the business' potential for success, and often the only way they would consider making an investment to guarantee an acceptable return on their money.

So what are my possible exit options?

Going Public: You can sell your company via the stock market in an initial public offering or IPO. An IPO allows investors to easily liquidate their investment and is a highly attractive exit strategy if the plan can demonstrate growth to a large enough company to warrant an IPO exit. The good news is that you stand the chance to get the biggest dollar payout of any other exit strategy. The bad news is that it is very expensive to manage an IPO, and you can easily spend up to millions of dollars on attorneys, accountants, and other fees. In addition, there are a lot of restrictions to achieving liquidity through an IPO. If your business is outside of the tech sector and has less than $50 million in revenues, generally you should consider a different strategy.

Merger: A merger is defined as two companies getting together, establishing a value for each company, and then combining the two to form one bigger company. In most mergers, the company shareholders receive stock in the larger pre-merger company which is presumably worth more than the stock held in each independent company. Therefore, be aware that in a merger, you may not actually receive cash for some time, certainly not during the merger itself. There are many times where having the resources of both companies creates a more valuable entity. However, mergers usually result in less control for the smaller entity, as you cede some power to the bigger company's management.

Sale: Selling your company is the most common exit strategy for business owners – to someone else or to some other company. For the most part it entails a transaction that can be conducted between two private parties without all the government regulations and oversight that occurs with an IPO unless you are selling to a public company. A sale typically results in the seller of the company receiving cash in exchange for the company shares or assets. The tricky part of any sale is valuing the company. Since most small businesses are privately held, the ultimate transaction price in a sale is sometimes more art than science. Make sure you get more than one appraisal of the business so that you have confidence that the price is right. This exit option allows you to completely sever your ties with your business, unless you and the buyer agree to equity in the acquiring company as part of your proceeds, which usually occurs as part of a transition period to keep the seller on board for a period of time to guarantee a smooth transition.

Buyout: Buyouts come in many flavors including Management Buyout (MBO) and leveraged buyout (LBO) to name a few. If another company comes in and takes over your business, you're being bought-out.

Typically, the buyer would be another company or individual with experience in the same line of work and who will take over your business on the basis of buying out your ownership. These transactions are often tied to the business performance at the time of the buyout and shortly after you leave. Sellers usually hope that the acquiring company pays the entire purchase price upfront. Buyers want some or much or the purchase price to be dependent upon continued performance of the company.

Another way of paying for the business could be based on what is known as a Leveraged Buyout (LBO), where the buyer leverages the future cash of the business to pay off their debt to you assumed as part of the purchase price. In other words, the assets of your company are used to borrow against in order to pay for the purchase, adding debt to the company after the sale, and increasing its interest expense and risk of ultimate survival.

A Management Buyout (MBO) is when managers and/or employees buy out your interests in the business. Just like another company buying out the business, the management buyout can be arranged either with a cash option, an LBO, or a combination of both. An important advantage of the MBO is that the buyers have been and will continue to be familiar with the business, customers, employees and vendors, thereby making for a smoother transition.

Succession: Keeping the business in the family could be attractive if you have willing and able family members. Keys to a successful family succession include properly preparing both the family member as well as the business for the transition. Family succession must be planed years in advance with ample of time reserved for training your future owners. In order to provide as much training as possible, individuals involved in the succession should be given tasks and responsibilities in all of the business aspects of the company rotating between all departments so that experience and knowledge can be gained across all major business activities. Common challenges associated with this option include potential family tensions, decisions made with emotion rather than reason, tax implications, and the possibility that you may not be able to cash out if part of the purchase price is in the form of a promissory note dependent upon the profits of the ongoing business.

Shutting Down: You can gain some amount of liquidity by shutting down the business and selling the assets (in asset liquidation). The major challenge is to be able to find buyers who feel that the business assets have value, and for you to be able to negotiate a fair price for those assets, some of them intangible and difficult to value. With this kind of exit strategy, you would usually be getting the smallest amount of money because you are selling the raw assets and finding intangible assets such as customer list worth almost nothing.

Although this option may seem to be the easiest because it requires little negotiation and no transfer of control, it can be the most emotional. When you close your business, there can be feelings of loss and little financial reward. However, this option may be the most reasonable if your business is highly dependent on you, if you are faced with an unexpected change in health, or if the economy or other circumstances make it impractical to seek out an alternative exit. Your business's legal structure will influence how to close down with the least amount of financial and legal implications. Sole proprietorships can simply cease operations and pay off any outstanding liabilities. However, there are other conditions to consider if you are operating as a partnership, a limited liability company or a corporation.

Regardless of your exit strategy, it is imperative that you have the right team of advisors on your side to guide you through the process. These include accountants, attorneys, investment bankers, or others who are experienced and have "seen the movie before." Except for shutting down your business and liquidating its assets, valuation of your business becomes the most important aspect when it comes to an exit. It is highly recommended to have all your finances and accounting in order and hire qualified valuation professionals to assist you in this process.

Accurate assumptions lead to defendable plans.

The biggest error in planning may not be spreadsheet calculation error. Or cost estimation. It is most often missed assumptions about the market, the competition, the speed of adoption, or other critical metrics you've researched, or selected, or even just guessed at to create your plan.

Where did you get the data to drive your assumptions of market size or market share? Most entrepreneurs quote a resource for market size, but fail to then take the next step to eliminate all parts of that market unreachable by the company or product. For example, if you supply software to the chip design industry, do you segment your market into digital and analog users, into high end or inexpensive buyers, and into which languages or platforms users demand or request?

It's easy to find someone to quote a size of market estimate. I became something of my industry's source for such a number when I carefully catalogued the 160 players both domestic and international, estimated revenues from knowing the number of employees or installations for each (which were often public knowledge or stated by those companies.) I then created a gross domestic and gross international annual market size estimate for my industry's products. No-one challenged this number, and it became an unattributed source of the metric for market size for years. Perhaps there was no other way to project the size of that market. But many decisions were made within my company walls, and surely by competitors, based upon those numbers.

Then there is the famous entrepreneur's statement about market share: "All I need to sell is one percent of the total available market to make this a rampant success." We call that the "gloves in China" syndrome when analyzing assumptions within business plans. Without a trace of how the business will get that one percent, the entrepreneur confidently shows that this is all it takes to make us all rich. Even if the total number of annual units in a market is known, the leap to a percent of that market without a specific plan is often a fatal one.

And these are just two of the many assumptions that underlie any business plan. At the very least, all assumptions should be driven by numbers separately listed in an "assumptions section" of the planning spreadsheet, allowing the reader to manipulate those assumptions to see the various outcomes, and challenge the numbers for the benefit of all who have to defend them.

Include your labor value in your plan.

Investors love it when entrepreneurs draw little or no money from their startups. It extends the cash available for research and other necessary fixed costs and gives the fragile, young company more "runway" to get to breakeven.

But when forecasting the ultimate viability of a business, many times an entrepreneurial founder uses a low, unsustainable salary rate for him or herself in order to show early breakeven. And that is the quandary for investors. If you had to replace yourself with a professional hired to duplicate your skills, what would you have to pay in salary and incentive today? That amount is almost always higher, much higher, than the amount budgeted for the entrepreneur.

You could start by charging more for your executive salary, then paying out less in cash, accruing the rest into a payable amount due to the entrepreneur. But that is a messy way to demonstrate that you are taking less than market wages from your company. Ultimately, the accrued difference will amount to a large enough liability that several things could happen, all of them negative.

The IRS could see that you are not paying yourself interest on the accrued debt, and consider it invested capital, eliminating your ability to repay yourself in the future. Worse yet, the IRS would then consider the accrued amount to be taxable income upon which no tax was paid, since the accrued labor as an investment has value that was not accounted for from previously taxed earnings. Or you could voluntarily convert the loan into stock with a single journal entry and a stock certificate. But the tax effect would be the same if audited – you would owe tax on the booked value.

The solution is to explain to potential investors that you are projecting under-market wages for the founder(s) for a period of time, perhaps until breakeven, and then to agree with them that you will move to market rate at that time.

My dad said: "Never take on a business partner."

My dad was a smart businessman, even if not formally trained. He occasionally gave me advice that turned out to be more than wise, looking back at subsequent experience and events. His personal teaching event was a typical experience, as I reflect now upon the tens of partnerships I have counseled over the years. Most often, one partner remained active as another partner drifted away from the business, no longer carrying the weight anticipated at start-up.

It's just one – the most prevalent – of the many things that can happen to well-meaning partners after time changes plans, and after the business passes through phases of growth or contraction.

I recall one very personal situation when I was very young, that reinforces Dad's advice. Through my college years, I managed a phonograph record production and manufacturing business that I created as a senior in high school, using independent contractors in local venues to record and edit the original tapes from recording musicals and performances from schools, colleges, churches and organizations throughout the USA and Canada - and then to sell the records to the appropriate audiences.

It grew to significant size during my college years, and I associated myself with a "strategic partner" throughout those years, ceding to him all recording and editing of work throughout the large home territory, and any national jobs we received. The agreement was that he would retain all of the revenues generated from those activities. We called ourselves "partners" and received lots of press, even nationally, as we managed our teenage business.

A year after graduation from college, I left for six months to serve my active duty obligation in the US Navy, while others took care of accounting and customer relations. And my "partner" left the company without notice and set up a competing company in my absence, never saying a word to any of us. I was bitter, but unable to do anything about it, since there was no partnership agreement. Luckily, after my return from active duty, my company flourished and his remained a small, one person operation for the rest of its existence. But, as they say, everything he learned, he learned from me. Dad was right, even if I learned the lesson years later.

So pay attention to the next two insights, authored by Richard Sudek and JJ Richa, in which our guest authors addresses the issues with a checklist of "how to" items that will help assure a successful partnership...

The five C's of Business Partners: a marriage without the sex
By Richard Sudek

Richard Sudek is an associate professor of entrepreneurism at Chapman University Graduate School of Business, is Director of the Leatherby Center for Entrepreneurism and Business Ethics, and Chairman Emeritus of the Tech Coast Angels, the largest angel group in the United States.

In working with entrepreneurs over the years, I have learned that the difference between success and failure is often centered on the people aspects of the business rather than strategy, finance, or operations. It is not that strategy, finance, and operations are not important, but rather failure of the business is more likely attributed to people issues. Nowhere is this more evident than with the issues related to business partners. Thinking about a business partnership like a marriage might be helpful in how you go about selecting a business partner.

You are likely to spend more time with your business partner than your spouse in the early stages of launching a business. This relationship may last 5-20 years. In many ways having a business partner is like getting married. You will spend a lot of time with that person (many years), you are likely to have employees (similar to having kids), you are likely to have arguments (but no make-up sex), you are likely to compromise (will not always win each fight), and the breakup can be messy and expensive (divorce court). When you look at it this way, you may want to spend some extra time considering how to select a business partner. Thus, when thinking about partnerships I suggest you think of the 5 C's: *Confidence, Competency, Complementary, Compatibility*, and *Contract.* Let's start with confidence, since this is about you rather than your partner.

Confidence is the first "C" because it refers to the confidence you have to launch your business. Sometimes an entrepreneur picks a partner because they experience some insecurity. This can range from emotional immaturity to functional insecurity. For instance, a good friend who now is in his 60s and was a very successful entrepreneur said he picked his first partner because he was insecure about his knowledge of finance. He felt he needed someone to compensate for this. It turned out that he really only needed a good bookkeeper and CPA. This partnership did not work well since the partner did not have much else to offer.

This might be the toughest "C" for younger entrepreneurs to deal with since it is really about self-assessment and introspection. How well do you really know yourself? Know your limitations? Your strengths? Ability to admit your weaknesses? You need to ask the question: Why do I need a partner? Is this what the business really needs? Or is this what I need? If what you need and the business needs are not the same, you might be seeking a partner for the wrong reason. Seek advice from mentors and other entrepreneurs who have been down this path before.

Competency is related to assessing a potential partner. The more experience you have the more you learn how to assess competency in others. This can range from a functional area such as marketing, or a people attribute like trust. Again, many younger entrepreneurs simply do not have the experience to do this well. This is when asking for help is important. The same entrepreneur who picked the wrong partner in the previous paragraph said now he would have multiple people interview a potential person, perform more due diligence on their background, and be much more thorough. When he was younger, he had too much arrogance to ask for help. The older you get, the less you worry about what you know, and focus more on what is the best way to get what you need.

Complementary is for picking a partner with complementary skills. Most of us think of this in functional areas, however, this is not the only area to seek complementary skills. It is important not to have significant overlap. For instance, if you are good at marketing, don't select a partner with a good marketing background. Find someone with technology, operations, manufacturing, or finance experience. Ask yourself, what skill does the business absolutely need?

But more importantly, are you complementary enough with this person to help make a complete CEO? Some of us act quickly and don't think deeply. Some act slowly but think deeply. Some of us are more enthusiastic, or volatile, or quiet. The worst thing you can do is find someone similar in personality and functional areas. Two technologists who are introverted are unlikely to make a good partnership. Steve Jobs and Steve Wozniak were a great example of being very different, yet these differences made for a very effective partnership.

Compatibility is related to how similar partners are on the dimensions of work ethic, integrity, style, and eventual outcome of the business or the exit among other issues. This is more of a personal fit issue rather than a functional fit. In other words - are you both going to work 100 hours a week in the beginning? When one partner feels they are putting more effort into the business, it is likely that resentment will build over time. Is how you frame integrity - and how you view different difficult choices that involve ethical issues similar? Something as simple as how to lay-off an employee and how much severance to offer can create significant disconnect with partners.

One time I was brought in to coach two partners. They had raised over a half million dollars, had fifteen employees, and thought they had strategic planning issues. What they had was a relationship problem. I ended up doing more couples counseling than CEO coaching or strategy work. They had never had the "exit" talk. They had not decided how or when they were going to exit, and what their personal dollar goal was for an exit. Be sure your personal issues related to the business have been discussed and are compatible.

Contract is the last "C" and might seem the most obvious. Every partnership needs to have a partner agreement, or in marriage terms, a pre-nup. Do you know exactly how you are going to part ways if things do not go as you plan, or if you simply want to get out? Do you know how you are going to value the company, how long it will take to pay the amount, and what the penalties are if you are late in paying? Worse yet, what if your partner dies and you are stuck (both legally and emotionally) with the remaining spouse who does not know anything about the business or industry? Marriage is till death-do-you-part, but business partnerships include what happens after death. The problem with this level of detail is that it can be an uncomfortable discussion for most. Consider hiring a third party to walk you through this. Since that person should not have ulterior motives, as is more likely to ask the very difficult questions about what might appear to be an unlikely scenario questions.

Selecting a partner is sometimes necessary, and extremely difficult. Few of us are complete CEOs. So spend the time and energy to make the best decision you can. Ask for help to assess potential partners and to dig into personal values and issues. And *always* have a contract.

Dave's note: After reading Richard Sudek's Five C's above, here is a detailed checklist from JJ Richa to use in creating and managing a successful partnership. - DWB

How to make a business partnership a success
By JJ Richa

Business partnerships have their advantages and disadvantages. Taking on a business partner is like a entering into a marriage. In general, partnerships are easy to get into and difficult to get out of. Certain guidelines should be taken into consideration along with a path to follow – from dating to pre-nup to marriage – all of which can be applied to a business partnership.

Taking on a business partner can be an excellent strategic decision in helping move the business forward. It should be well thought out for all parties involved. The relationship needs to be synergistic financially, emotionally, and operationally. All parties need to perform due diligence to ensure that the assumptions are correct, that neither partner has financial issues which could affect the partnership, and that the opposite partner has the skills to contribute to the partnership.

Most of the important benefits for partnering include:

- Combining of complimentary skill sets
- Access to new markets
- Addition of new services or product lines
- Addition of essential expertise and knowledge to propel the business forward
- Open doors to new distribution channels
- Access to new technologies
- Access to capital unavailable to either partner singly

Certain steps should be taken before entering into a partnership.

1. Personal assessment and getting to know one another:

   - Work together on 2-3 projects before an agreement is consummated
   - Determine the commitment of the potential partners. Is the potential partner in for the long haul?
   - Identify each of the partner's unique contribution. Does the potential partner bring specialized knowledge, skills, leadership, or experience that compliments others?
   - Understand each person's personal goals. Are each set of goals consistent with the other's including for example personal wealth, business success, and autonomy?

- Determine trust and Values. Is there trust between the parties? Do the proposed partners share a set of common values? Core values are none negotiable. Be ready to walk away when others are willing to negotiate their own values or try to negotiate others.

2. Determine personal and business goals:

- Contribution: What will the new partner contribute? Example: cash, assets, equipment, connections… Regardless of what it is, a partner's contribution needs to increase the value of the business.
- Compensation: What are compensation expectations? Example: salary, equity, joint venture, etc… Can the business afford it?
- Control: What type of control is the new partner looking for? Example: percent of ownership, officer/operational, director/board member… What are the parties willing to give up in return for the prospect of business success?
- Brand and Success: Is the new partner dedicated to ensuring brand continuity and contribute to the success, or just to ride on what has been established by the other?

3. Create roles and guidelines in the potential partnership:

- What role and responsibility will each of the partners have including operation, financial, sales, marketing, etc..?
- How will decisions be made and by whom? Is it by committee?
- Will each have certain level of decision making authority? Will the new process impair quick decision making?
- Will authority limits be defined, and processes and procedures put in place?
- What is the understanding if one of the partners wants out or wants more? What is the understanding if things go downhill/uphill?

4. Perform preliminary due diligence:

- Review the business plan including marketing, sales strategies and financial needs

- Review long term company debt, goals, objectives and financial projections
- Review financial statements – up to 3 years if available
- Review tax returns - up to 3 years if available
- Research and talk to existing and past customers

5. Create partnership agreement basic terms:

- Define Key Performance Indicators (KPIs.) How will the success of the business be measured?
- Clarify decision making and dispute resolution processes
- Define each partner's title and position
- Define management responsibilities and job descriptions
- Detail authority limits for each partner
- Clarify operation responsibilities and metrics used to measure performance
- Define vacations and time off policies such as with partners vacationing at the same time
- Determine compensation for each partner
- Exit strategy planning, including determining what happens when one partner leaves, if closing the business, if selling the business, creating a mutual buy/sell agreement, and more.

Depending on the legal structure of the business, different types of formal agreements may be required.

Partnership agreement should never be 50/50 regardless of the perception of compatibility at the time of execution. There must be some method of resolving a tie that is predetermined in the agreement.

Potential partners should follow and apply these guidelines independently. This should be followed by a joint meeting to determine commonalities, synergies, and conflicts. If necessary, this is the time to bring in an impartial third party to facilitate any possible conflicts and resolutions.

It is highly recommended that legal document are created and/or reviewed by a business transaction attorney. All agreements should be in writing and signed by all parties involved. Regardless of what method is taken to reach an agreement among partners, avoid some of the common mistakes. These include premature rejection of ideas by the other partner, prematurely judging others, one-sided financial consideration, and not sticking to core values.

Build a company - not just a product.

Some businesses are built around a single idea. And sometimes that idea is just too small a slice of the big picture to be interesting to investors. There was a recent investor event where I was keynote speaker, on stage only after several panels of experts had wowed the audience with their predictions and observations. One of the panelists made a point that resonated with me.

She stated that she had rejected the investment being discussed, because in her mind the entire company was "just a button, on a feature, in an app." That comment sent me thinking about relevance, about longevity, and about market size for some of these entrepreneurial applicants looking for funding.

If you have invented a game that will be marketed as a new app in the app store, have you created enough of a model to create an ongoing company, or just another app that will compete with the hundreds of thousands already in the store? Is your game using a unique engine, or series of animated characters, or method of play that will break ground with potential players, inducing them to look to you for more and more unique games over time?

Far too many companies have been created around a button on a feature, and not upon a solution to a need in answer to a void in the market. Investors have seen this game before. We match what we see to what has succeeded for us in the past. And rarely do we see a plan for a single product that is not part of a larger vision, and remain interested long enough to ask for more information.

There are exceptions. The famously popular app, "Draw It," might at first seem an exception, until you dig deeper to find a dense plan around a series of social engagement products planned to follow. Can you extend your product into a planned series? Plan to create apps, not buttons, and not features.

Ready, aim, fire. Really?

You've surely heard the variations on this theme. "Ready, fire aim" was popular in the 1990's, accredited to any of several authors. I used the term to describe my efforts in the artificial intelligence field, experimenting with new devices, the lisp programming language, and our first trial installations. It seemed an ideal way to describe a scrappy, entrepreneurial activity.

So why do so many business-book authors stress the opposite behavior? Ready, FIRE, aim. What happens to careful planning, sure-fire metrics, quality test scenarios, market research, a good business plan – all in place before pulling the trigger of a new opportunity.

And who is right here?

If you're seeking investment from anyone other than friends and family, you're probably going to have to navigate through the exercise of careful planning, documentation and execution. Investors are a fickle bunch in general. They want to know that their money is not just being thrown at an idea that will become a trial by fire – literally.

On the other side of the argument is the truth of the claim that numerous iterations in the form of rapid prototypes and execution of new ideas in the field quickly refine the product or service to meet the needs of the customer, and at a far faster and cheaper pace than with careful pre-planning.

In the software arena, there is a term for this: "cowboy coding." Without the need to carefully document the architecture and elements of a proposed application, a single programmer can much more quickly just code, test, and create revised code. Without even pausing to document the process internally, no-one can easily take over the job, if for any reason the cowboy coder is no longer in control. And the result? Typically, we call that "spaghetti code" to signify code that is so often changed that it no longer looks clean and traceable.

The conclusion is that the best process depends upon the product, its critical core nature to the business using it, and the way in which the entrepreneur approaches the need for outside investors.

Critical components of any operation or business must be carefully constructed, tested and inserted into the operation of the business.   On the other hand, if a new free iPad app has bugs, they can be corrected in the next automatic update, and probably without much customer noise.

Which is better for you: rapid iteration or careful planning? What is your case for defending your method of creating new products or services?

The three step dance

Creating a new company in a relative vacuum is an exercise in complete trust that the entrepreneur knows what's best for the customer, perhaps even without interaction with such a customer. It's probably happened, but not often enough to trust this method as a formula for success.

So, I've developed *the three step dance* in order to help form a repeatable method of how to create a great company from an early idea.

The first step: *Involve potential customers early*. Even if you know it all - wouldn't it be an excellent plan to try your idea out on enough actual or potential customers to measure reasonable feedback?

You can use or discard the information you receive. We now know that Steve Jobs created in relative secrecy several of his products that became massive industry drivers of change. The iPad probably would have failed before production, had he used feedback and research from past failures of tablets in any previous form as a guide. On the other hand, most products or services are created in response to a real or perceived need. And most of us are not Steve Jobs.

The second step: *Take feedback seriously*. Making the effort to gather metrics from the field in any form and then ignoring it, takes guts and determination - and in most cases a measure of stupidity. As I analyze business plans, I usually ask the entrepreneur early in the process whether s/he has tried this idea or prototype or mockup out on potential users. And if so, what was the response? And from how many people? In what related universe? I want to know that potential paying customers have been queried using enough information or a good enough model to get a real response worth taking seriously. Without this, any information received is suspect. And failure to make use of the information is a red flag for investors.

The third step: *Reiterate and return to customers for comments*. Seeking, then analyzing responses allows you to make changes to the plan and product in response. But what if the changes create other problems for the customer, or miss the mark, or don't drive these same customers to more positive responses? The best possible second round feedback should come from the very same people who took the time to review the offering the first time. They have context and should see effort and progress. Their comments should therefore be more valued than those from first-time respondents.

The three step dance:

1. Involve your customers early.

2.   Take feedback seriously.
3.   Reiterate and return to customers for comments.

So, why not design your product using your real and potential customers as consultants?

Eyeballs aren't everything.

Back when we were all trying to figure out the real value of traffic on the web, we investors - and acquiring companies - got a bit crazy with metrics used to value acquisitions and investments. Since in most cases, there was no revenue in many of these companies, all trying to gain market share at any cost, we had to invent the metric to use. And the most logical one seemed to be "eyeballs" or number of unique users finding their way to the site or registering for the service.

And the numbers were staggering. Microsoft paid $9.00 per registered user for Hotmail. AOL paid $40.00 per registered user of ICQ, the early messaging service. I was the original investor and helped to grow GameSpy Industries, attracted to the fledgling company because of its million users each month, even though at the time there was no monetization to the traffic.

But, when the bubble burst in 2000, most of us quickly grew up. Revenue models became more important a measure than traffic, although market share was and still is an over-weighted part of the value of any Internet-based entity.

That is the quandary which entrepreneurs face today in building models for new companies around a web presence.   Great revenue projections from a small user base lead to worries over sustainability. Low revenue projections but demonstrated (or projected) impressive numbers of unique users lead investors to think that there may be a future method of monetizing the user base that makes the company attractive, even while currently losing money.

I am an investor and advisor to one such company. Gaining users at a rate of 50% a month, the company has yet to find a revenue model that will pay for the increased costs of infrastructure needed to support the growth, let alone the fixed cost of operating the enterprise. And yet, users rave about the service, and spend long durations of time on the site.

Once we had what we thought was the answer, in allowing for display advertising on these sites. But the competition among sites has overwhelmed available inventory of paying advertisers, greatly reducing the cost per thousand views, and making display ads no longer a preferred revenue source for marginal sites.

We experimented with subscription-based charges for game sites and other sites supplying what we thought were indispensable services. In every case, those subscription models failed, as users found free alternatives. One of my companies had four million free beta gamers registered on the site, but lost all but 10,000 when attempting to charge $9.95 a month for a subscription.

What is the answer? New forms of advertising have been created to force user views, including pop-ups, pre-roll ads containing video content, and click-through display ads before allowing content views. Major newspapers and magazines, trying to reinvent themselves, are using the subscription model, as well as all of the above methods in their attempt to become relevant to a new and growing mobile and Internet-focused user base, with varying - but not too satisfying results.

Micropayments, in which services and information are delivered for pennies, requires an infrastructure for collecting, accumulating and billing that is still being experimented with, but showing promising results.

Giants like Facebook and Google have such large eyeball numbers that they can use display and positioning ads to achieve great profits. Most of us are still searching for the combination of monetization devices that work best for us. Free sites without monetization will disappear over time, and we will lose services we take for granted today. It is in the best interest of both Internet users *and* providers to find an acceptable way to charge for valuable services or information.

It's mostly in the execution.

"Everybody's got a plan - until they are punched in the face," stated boxer Mike Tyson. My experience personally reviewing over three hundred executive summaries each year, all sent to me unsolicited, seems to bear out the truth in Tyson's statement. Anyone can build a good – or great – plan. Investors have to look behind the plan and at the entrepreneur and his or her team, knowing that, over time, most of us have come to the conclusion that it is the execution of the ever-changing plan, not the plan itself that makes a company a success.

Tyson's statement also addresses change. The 'punch in the face' is analogous to dealing with the business plan when it intersects with the realities of the market. Wham! I can't recall any of my companies hanging onto its original plan after some level of consumer feedback.

We built one of our companies upon forecasted metrics for a specific class of retail consumer base, but found that there wasn't enough money in our universe to pay for marketing to create that much dedicated traffic to our site. So we switched to distribution through partners which already had massive amounts of traffic, and concentrated in providing great content and great offers that more than made up for the sharing of revenues.

There is a name for such a change in focus, in this case from retail to wholesale. We call it a "pivot," a term now used to describe great management dealing with successfully refocusing a company in a new direction.

And most of us who invest in so many companies have come to the conclusion that our greatest profits over time come from investments in great management, groups that we are confident are able to execute even on average plans. Some label this as "Bet on the jockey, not the horse."

Burn the bridges behind.
By Frank Peters

Frank Peters made his money writing software for Wall Street. Today he is best known as the host of the Frank Peters Show, delivered via the web each week to tens of thousands of entrepreneurs, angels and VCs worldwide. Frank speaks and networks at angel events around the world.

I became an entrepreneur because I had to. My life in Corporate America wasn't going so well. I never got fired, but I did quit one job the day before I was to be let go. I used my employee discount that last day to purchase a Compaq luggable computer and drove with my brother to Las Vegas. Now, this would be questionable therapy for anyone who just became unemployed, except we were heading to *Comdex*, the annual computer show that would eventually grow huge as would the industry itself. I consider this trip the anniversary of the company's starting up, and made the trip 11 years in a row.

How was striking out on my own? I'd often say: "I created the company so no one could fire me." I never took a business course, never wrote a business plan, and never raised any outside capital.

As I look back at insights I might share, I wade through the trite suggestions of 'work hard' and 'treat the customer well.' But there's more. *Burn the bridges behind* comes to mind. I had no alternatives to success. I was not going back to corporate America. It wasn't a fall- back position. I had to be successful at my new software company. And it wasn't easy.

I remember taking a walk with my wife one evening and sharing my concerns over cash flow. My sales tax payments were due in the next few days, and I didn't have the money. Default would bring many consequences. But I did have an appointment, a sales opportunity the next morning. I woke up that next morning with a jolt - literally. An earthquake struck Los Angeles. In an hour I received a phone call from the friend who was in the office where I was due later that morning. He had made the introduction for my appointment. "People are pretty shook up here today. Some were stuck in an elevator. I don't know if today's the best day to come up." He wasn't telling me I couldn't come, so, because I had to, I did. I made the sale, and paid my debts. I always remember that 'back against the wall' feeling. It was stressful and yet so typical when running a small company.

This morning over coffee, my wife told me of a dream she had last night. It was about the earliest days of our life together when we moved to Westwood so I could attend UCLA. "Moving out west away from our families was one of the best things that could've happened to us at that early age," she recalled wistfully. "We had to make a go of it." It brought back the memories of landing at LAX in 1974 with three suitcases and $1,900 to our names. Like my eventual experience as an entrepreneur, we had to persevere. We had no alternatives. *We had burned our bridges behind.*

How many innovations are carefully planned?

Most innovations come from responding to a customer's needs, or finding a niche where products need improvement or extension. It is rare to innovate using a blank sheet of paper in a room with bare walls and no other contributors.

Imagine the room in which several graduate business school student groups have gathered, tasked with coming up with an idea for a business plan competition. The group starts with a blank sheet, and toils through idea after idea, trying to come up with a product or service that might become the next FedEx. That is tough work, and not a very productive way to start a process. Sometimes, the result is spectacular. Most of the time, this form of thinking produces a plan that requires real work to imagine success.

I'd advise the students to do it differently. I'd advise them to pick a growing industry. Then find a short list of users, customers, and consultants in that industry who are known to be advanced in their thinking as demonstrated by their prior work. Then I'd advise them to visit the CEO. And ask, "What is it that bothers you most about your operation?" "What is you biggest problem, other than working capital?" "Where's your bottleneck in production or sales or development?" "If you could invent a solution, what would it be?"

Now that's how to find pain in an industry. And yet, few think to use this form of investigation. Yes, you can argue that probably Fred Smith might not have thought of FedEx if he had just interviewed rail or postal customers. But maybe someone would have given Smith the bare idea from which he could imagine a much bigger opportunity.

If you're starting a new company because you have a better way to do something, create something or market something, you have a head start. But if you're trying to think of what you want to produce, start with finding the pain in the marketplace, and set out to remove it.

Henry Ford famously said, "If I asked my customers what they wanted, they would have said 'a faster horse.'" As a mechanical genius, even that comment might have led Ford to envision a way to provide reliable, fast, inexpensive, mechanical horsepower. It is the process of leaping from a need to an eloquent solution that creates demand and ultimately success in the marketplace.

Management quality trumps a quality plan.

Great management teams mean more to investors than even greater business plans.

If flexibility and coachability are first in the list of traits investors value in an entrepreneur, then the quality of the proposed or actual management team come in a close second, even before the attractiveness of the business plan itself. The quest for a great management team is not a fluke, but rather a result of backward looks at the failure rate from past investments by angel investors and venture capitalists.

It is true that at least half of the businesses backed by professional early stage investors will die within three years or less. That reality is a tough one for the professional investor, almost as tough as for those entrepreneurs who lose their businesses.   The latter can start new businesses, flush with the experiences gained from the previous effort and much the better for it.   The investor's cash is lost forever, and the experience gained usually is just another increment in a list of similar experiences from the past.

It is the management team, most often led by a passionate entrepreneur with experience in the industry, which makes the biggest difference between success and failure, even for businesses built upon less than sterling basic ideas. Among professional investors, almost all would rather back a great team with an average idea before a great idea and inexperienced team. It comes back to coachability and flexibility, our first insight. Great teams are flexible and have the advantage of experience in seeing the pitfalls before them from their past. They are coachable in that they have taken advantage of the vast experience of others in overcoming obstacles and finding ways to speed a product to market faster or create a service whose quality exceeds that of the competition.

None of this is to say that an inexperienced entrepreneur cannot lead a great new business.   But it would be foolish to try without surrounding himself with as many experienced co-leaders as possible from the outset. As a start, such an entrepreneur will soon "know what he (she) doesn't know", an important qualifier for success in any business endeavor, when combined with the willingness to fill gaps in knowledge with help from those who have the experience to do so.

Ask any professional investor, and you should hear that they value the quality of the team above the attractiveness of the early drafts of the business plan.   Even without taking in money from professional investors, that advice would serve you well in protecting your own monetary investment.

Trade secrets + customer lists = company gold.

Don't take from others and don't let others take yours.

We must pause in this journey toward building an overwhelmingly successful business with an admonition that may seem obvious to some and completely sail over the heads of others. Most entrepreneurs arrive at the starting line of a new business with a vision for the future and some degree of experience from the past. Often, that experience comes from being employed within a business that was similar, but whose senior management may have missed or deliberately ignored what the entrepreneur sees as a great opportunity.

And most senior and middle level managers will understand when a subordinate comes to them to resign and begin a new business. But all will immediately question whether the new business will compete in any way with their enterprise, and react to the future entrepreneur in either of two very distinct ways based upon those fears.

If the employee who is about to resign is off to conquer the world in a completely new arena, there is almost always the unspoken sigh of relief and a cooperative attitude that flows from the senior manager from that point on in the conversation.

But if the employee is even a little bit reticent to tell of the plan envisioned, the result is the first stage of what could become an outright war between the present employer and a newly separated past employee, sent away that day with an escort out the door.

The same attitudes from past employers can be expected if a past employee resurfaces after a layoff, resignation or after being fired, with a plan for a competitive business. Most employers have all their employees sign non-disclosure and confidentiality agreements to protect the company's trade secrets, customer lists and business plans. Many states recognize the right of a former employee to work, even if in direct competition with a past employer. But that right clearly stops when the entrepreneur uses any trade secret data from the past employer, especially customer lists for contacts and confidential business plans as bases for new businesses.

Anyone can be sued even if without merit, and responding to a suit can be traumatic in many ways – from expenditure of cash and valuable time to emotional drain from worry over a negative outcome, to loss of industry goodwill by an entrepreneur perceived to have stepped over the line.

This is especially true for someone who has sold a business only to surface later to compete in some way with the buyer. Never underestimate the venomous response from such a threat.

So no matter what your circumstance, never, ever be guilty of using trade secret materials or ideas from your past employer, especially customer lists.

Watch out for the gray areas in non-competes.

What if you are the seller of a previous business or shares amounting to more than an insignificant percentage of a previous business? Certainly the buyer's asset purchase documents included a non-compete clause, usually valid for two years from the date of the closing. And because there was consideration paid to you in the sale, that clause is binding upon you and is effective almost everywhere.

Well, what if the buyer is now bankrupt? That does nothing to regain your right to its purchased information. The estate of the bankrupt company retains and can resell those rights into the infinite future. (Patents expire after 14 or 20 years – depending upon type - and publicly disclosed patent information is no longer subject to the agreements after that expiration, as long as you use only the publicly disclosed information as filed within the patents themselves.)

What if the buyer abandons your previous product? That does not change their purchased rights to it. What if you invent a substantial enhancement or change to the product? As long as you did not use patented processes or trade secret material from you previous company, you should be protected, but you might be prepared for a fight.

How about after the two year limitation in your agreement? Separate confidentiality from non-compete, and obey the confidentiality clauses. The non-compete agreement does expire when stated. But watch it. Some clever buyers try to slip in an unlimited non-compete, and some courts have upheld this. And there are gray areas for former key employees who signed a non-compete with a limited life as part of the sale, but remained on for some time thereafter employed by the buyer. Does the non-compete start anew upon the employee's departure? Courts tend to apply only the reasonableness standard to these gray area cases, looking to see how much the person now competing gained from the original sale.

The safest advice is to avoid using any materials from the previous company, and compete only after the expiration of any written agreements or clauses signed with the buyer.

Vision is everything.

I love absolute statements. And this is one of my favorites. You're at the ignition stage of a new business venture. Of course you have a vision for what that business will do to change the world. And this insight is directed to you in an attempt to stress test that vision and sharpen it further to help insure your success.

Let me address those whose vision may be limited and who will be happy with a successful local dry cleaning enterprise or small restaurant around the corner. Although many of these insights will help you succeed, you are not the target for this epic effort to help entrepreneurs build great businesses that do change the world. Take what you can from these bursts of insight. I wish you well in your endeavors.

For the rest of you who want to change the world, I am with you and happy to offer all the help I can to reinforce your opportunities for success.

To you, let me repeat: vision is everything. A great vision for a new enterprise drives innovation. It serves as the rallying cry for all future employees, investors, customers and even suppliers. It sharpens the understanding of those new to the enterprise and moves them to follow and even to become unpaid advocates for the business.

Think of some of the great visions from the past that did change the world. "Absolutely, positively overnight" made FedEx an indispensible name in supply chain management. "A computer on every desk" made Microsoft a partner in the growth of most every business. You can think of many more, visions expressed so clearly that the enterprise became critical to your own success.

There are other, less dramatic ways to express a vision. "Be the largest supplier of laser toner in North America", or "Make dining into a five star experience."

Years ago, as a panelist at an entrepreneurial seminar, I watched as over fifty aspiring young entrepreneurs filed past a microphone, each tasked with making a thirty second pitch to the panelists of professional investors. About halfway through this painful exercise, one man walked up to the microphone and said, simply, "We move oil through the Internet" and then he moved on. Immediately after the panel presentation, I found that one entrepreneur and began a conversation that led to my investing $100,000 in his vision of a supply chain enterprise based upon perfect knowledge of oil delivery systems, precise timing of delivery and coordination of resources to move oil from source to customer using the Internet as a frictionless tool for communication and coordination.

Although that business ultimately failed, I still speak with that entrepreneur as he uses his experience in a new field, better off as a result of his learning experience. I carry no rancor as a result of the loss, since I bought into the vision, helped as I could with the execution, and came to the realization along with the entrepreneurial team that the number of uncontrollable elements far exceeded those which could be controlled by any third party at that stage of development of the Internet.

We will explore vision in more depth in recognition of its importance to success.

Address ten vision tests for success.

A vision must be solid and flexible enough to pass a number of critical tests if it is to guide a business enterprise to greatness. Here in brief are ten tests for a successful vision. Try these on for size, and test yourself for attractiveness to the marketplace, to investors and to history.

Ten tests for a successful vision

1. *Is your market identifiable and accessible?* Test yourself as to whether you can identify the size of your market niche, and whether you can overcome the many barriers to access customers within your niche.

2. *Where in industry life cycle?* If your vision is for a product or service that fills a need in a mature industry, you may be flying against the prevailing winds as a market shrinks over time, taking your business with it. Conversely, a fast growing industry lifts most all good participants, making excellent companies excel even more and grow even faster, like a small plane flying at 150 knots with a 75 knot tailwind.

3. *How large a total market?* If the total market for your niche is under $100 million per year, it is going to be difficult to build a $50 million business, even if not impossible. If the market is ten times that size, there is probably room for competitors to fight for dominance and still succeed if you are not number one.

4. *Can you dominate that market?* The dominant player in any niche controls pricing for all those under it, and often sets the risk profile for new entrants into the niche if the dominant player's products or services fill the needs of customers at reasonable prices and quality.

5. *Have you created high barriers to entry?* If your business is a "me too" entrant into any market niche, even the smallest

success will soon attract competitors that will sap some degree of your potential growth. What can you prove as a barrier to entry for competitors? Is it the advantage of time – years of development ahead of any competitor? A core patent or "thicket" of patents protecting your offering? A strategic relationship with one or more of the largest customers?

6. *Are margins high enough?* Some great ideas just can't make money and ultimately die for lack of profit potential. Profit margins are higher for unique products or services early in the life of an industry niche, or for products protected by patents that prevent others from undercutting you simply by releasing a cheaper product. High profit margins are a sign of high barriers to entry and attract investors and ultimately good buyers for your business.

7. *Can this business grow to above $50MM?* This is a basic test for investors, separating your business from those with smaller visions. There is nothing wrong with a vision for a smaller enterprise if not in need of professional investors to make it a reality.

8. *Do you have a world-class management team?* The best way to protect against failure is to attract a team with members who have experienced success and failure and can recognize the ways to manage toward success and avoid the pitfalls previously experienced from past failures. From a professional investor's perspective, the team should be able to be flexible, coachable and experienced enough to get a business through breakeven and beyond the next level of outside investment, greatly reducing execution risk.

9. *Can you translate an idea into a compelling product?* Some great ideas just cannot be made into a product at a reasonable enough prices to attract customers. And some attract early adopters but cannot pass into the mass market. Sometimes, an idea is just too early for the available technology to make it

attractive. Early cell phones were large bricks that required a large carrying case and cost up to a dollar a minute to use. As technology caught up, allowing miniaturization and light weight, mass adoption drove the price down and allowed the building of infrastructures everywhere to support the use of inexpensive minutes. Do anything you can to develop compelling products or early prototypes as proof of ability to reduce technology risk.

10. *Is there an exit strategy for the investor(s) over time?* There are many professional services businesses that make fine lifestyle opportunities for architects, doctors and dentists. But these types of businesses are not attractive to potential buyers willing to pay a premium for businesses that are worth millions more than their asset value. Building a great business to create wealth for the entrepreneur at exit, means thinking of the exit strategies from the beginning. Who or what type of buyer would be attracted to this business if successful? Great wealth is made from selling great businesses at immense profit for the entrepreneurs and investors who took the journey.

A compelling vision drives innovation.

Companies that innovate new products, services and methods of delivery are the ones that stand out in a crowded business world, especially when attempting to gain recognition beside competitors on the web.

Innovation is valued by our society, by investors and certainly by consumers. It is the focus for state and federal governments worldwide, many finding ways to reward innovators with tax incentives or investors with tax credits to finance innovative new enterprises.

As a keynote speaker, I often start presentations that start with a short history of innovation in the United States, using the twist of examining innovation through the lens of 150 years of cyclic bursts of bubbles, leading to subsequent recessions and depressions. It is not hard to find strands of gold in the carnage left by failed businesses lost when a bubble bursts, such as in 1857, 1902, 1929 and 2001.

Innovators make use of golden strands of opportunity left when the unfinished vision of another cries for completion, or when a genuine new concept changes the very way people think about their lives.

Leonard Kleinrock and a few of his UCLA computer lab students worked to send the first several characters from UCLA to Stanford in 1969 over a direct line established for the test. They were able to send only the "LO" of "LOGON" before recording the very first crash of the Internet. And I'm sure they had no idea what they were fathering with that effort which eventually became ARPANET, and then of course, the Internet itself. They had no mantra, and a limited vision to connect mainframe computers to share academic information.

How many entrepreneurs used that infrastructure to create an expansive vision of what could be? Tim Burners-Lee wanted to use this new infrastructure to create a friendlier web of pages, sharing data like the pages of a massive library of books extending throughout the world. The result was the worldwide web, upon which Mark Andreeson and his crew in Chicago built the Mosiac browser to make this data more available to anyone. Which in turn allowed innovators worldwide to create applications inside a browser, share detailed information previously locked inside libraries and corporations, and ultimately to change the world by making the exchange of information frictionless.

We can look back to Edison, Ford and Bell as great innovators of their time. But perhaps the most impressive invention of recent times is the result of hundreds of people, firms, and institutions, each adding a new brick to the building of the Internet.

Now we have the infrastructure for innovators to create applications with free software on computers used for many purposes simultaneously. And millions of innovators are at work extending the capabilities of the Internet.

What opportunities are next? Perhaps it is the remaking of the world through green technologies, clean technologies, new medical technologies, new home entertainment products, new mobile communications products and services, and more.

Who said that *"Everything that can be invented has been invented?"* Ah yes. That was Charles H. Duell, U.S. Commissioner of Patents in 1899. Oops.

Fewer words, greater effect.

I have a business friend, an experienced manager and teacher with a Harvard MBA, whose creativity and intelligence are admired by many. But he dilutes his effectiveness with wordy PowerPoint presentations. It has become a long running joke between us, as I often remind him that most of us have a very limited attention span and ability to recall important points from a presentation.

Note the title and tone of these insights. Short, to the point.

Mark Twain said, "I didn't have time to write a short letter so I wrote a long one instead." He cogently encapsulated the problem.

It is more difficult to reduce your thoughts to a few core sentences, but that is what you should do for maximum effect.

The trend is your friend.

Too many startup businesses, especially in the technology world, are built upon brand new concepts that have not yet been proven in the field with products from other companies that have revenues flowing. As a rule, creating a product that does not fit into an existing space, cannot be defined against one or more competitors, or which needs a long description to understand, will require considerably more marketing capital and entail much more risk than one that follows an existing trend, even if an emerging one.

I've often used the analogy of "flying against the prevailing winds" to prove this point. A pilot flying *with* the wind behind is helped by the speed of the wind and uses less fuel and less time to make it to the destination. One flying *into* the wind uses double the difference in both fuel (money) and time. For example, a 100 knot plane flying into a 50 knot headwind and using 8 gallons of fuel per hour uses *double the fuel*, (16 gallons) and takes *twice as long* to the destination as with no wind. If flying with the winds behind, the flight takes 66% of the fuel and gets to the destination is two thirds of the time as if with no winds.

That's a valuable lesson. If others have created awareness of the market, you need only compare yourself favorably to those companies. If the market is moving quickly toward your class of product or service, you may be able to gain a piece just by being there at the right time with the right product or service.

Either way, very few startups can afford to forge new markets or create a product that does not fit into an existing class of increasing demand.

I have often told the story of a company I financed and helped to found, back in the days of analog cell phones. People could not easily or cheaply carry their analog cell phones from city to city, often having no service or having to pay a dollar a minute for roaming service. Our company developed a unique product for hotels that allowed a guest to use a local cell phone provided by the hotel and make calls as if in the room even while traveling through the city, and to remotely receive calls made to the room phone in the hotel.

The problem was that our company did not see far enough ahead to know that digital cell phones and roaming plans were right around the corner. When they arrived, our expensive phone switches and analog phones were almost immediately obsoleted, as travelers quickly bought digital cell phones with roaming plans. The company had to take back all of its equipment at the end of each hotel's lease, and went out of business as a result. The question to ask: Didn't anyone know or have a friend who knew of the development and subsequent release of digital cell phones in the two years before they became a reality? Certainly there were resources available to point the company toward the information. The market was moving in the opposite direction from the company, and the company paid the ultimate price.

Fly with, not against the prevailing winds of change. The trend *is* your friend.

Is success a goal or a byproduct?

Look this up sometime in your browser: "Success is a byproduct, not a goal." You will find it attributed to tens of originators. I first heard this in an episode of *Friday Night Lights*, when sage Coach Taylor began a locker room speech with those words.

And yet, when I facilitate strategic planning sessions, I often lead executives to create a goal for their enterprise, one which can be reached by successfully accomplishing a series of strategic actions, each of which is braced with a series of tactics to accomplish in its support. The goal is often stated in revenues, such as "Become a twenty million dollar company in three years."

Achieving such a goal is a direct measure of the success of the company's strategies and tactics. But in this case, the goal *is* success, which is counter to the locker room speech by the good coach.

It is most important to focus everyone in the organization on a goal. And when that goal is achieved, another should be set, then another. Achievement of the goal is a byproduct of the successful accomplishment of each of those strategic and tactical actions called for in a good plan.

The point to remember is that you, as leader, must set and broadcast a clear goal, one that rallies your troops to succeed. Don't let the goal be achieved merely by the accident of good work and practice. Make it tangible, obvious, attainable with effort, and worthwhile for the players on your team. In that sense, success *is* a goal, contrary to the locker room encouragement by the coach.

The Fifty Percent Startup Rule.

Fifty percent of all businesses formed fail within the first two years.

There are many variations of this number since there are a number of ways to measure failure. But the number is a startling reminder that creating a business is not easy, nor is it any assurance of success.

After speaking with many entrepreneurs over the years, each defines success in his or her unique way. To some, it is independence from the dictates of a boss who doesn't appreciate that person's talent, foresight, or abilities. To some it is financial security, building a base of wealth created from the increased value of the enterprise at the end point of sale or at an IPO. To others, it is simply a way to express a talent for art, cooking, consulting, management, development or more.

Everyone has a vision when starting a business. And few think of the risks that increase over time as initial capital is expended. We all see the examples of well-known successful entrepreneurs, many in our chosen field, who achieve success by anyone's measure, and we optimistically expect to emulate these role models with at least some level of success.

The best advice to anyone considering this course of action is to measure one's ability to take the risk. That ability varies with economic status, age, responsibility to family, and more. If there is enough freedom to make that leap, then the journey can more safely begin. If not, there are alternatives, such as raising initial capital from friends and family, before leaving the life boat of a present job.

Some say that taking the leap, burning the bridges, the life boats - or whatever security is left behind - forces the entrepreneur to focus like never before and succeed because there is no alternative. Although investors may respect that bold a move, it is so dangerously risky as to be a bit insane. Then again, with the fifty percent rule, aren't all entrepreneurs a bit insane to start?

The Eighty Percent Acquisition Rule.

Eighty percent of all businesses purchased by another company or by a new investor-operator fail to meet the stated expectations of the buyer after one year.

As with the fifty percent rule, this rule is hard to find an author willing to be quoted as the source. But it is within the range of experience by many who have acted as brokers, serial purchasers or consultants for acquisitions.

With this rate of disappointment, why would anyone or any company purchase another? The answer is that the most sophisticated buyers have experience in integrating an acquisition successfully into an enterprise and those successes are the most visible models for others to follow. As we move down the chain of experienced buyers, the problems of underestimation of capital, customers who drifted away from the acquired company, key employees who found the new enterprise a culture too different to endure and left, and other difficult-to-plan-for events overwhelm the majority of acquired companies, resulting in less revenue, less profit, and far less growth than forecast during the buyer's due diligence.

There are great lessons to learn from Cisco and other companies that have grown wonderfully by acquisition, understanding the need to maintain elements of the acquired company's culture, while offering the employees retained new and attractive reasons to stay and build the combined enterprise.

So this insight is simple. Study the literature about companies that have succeeded in their acquisitions, finding how and why such successes rose to the top twenty percent of all acquisitions when measured by the acquiring company CEO satisfaction ratings after a year. Emulate the actions that are appropriate. Plan for surprises by keeping enough capital available to restart or re- align the acquired company after an initial problem period.

Over all, know the eighty percent rule and act carefully to protect both the acquirer and the entity acquired against failed expectations.

Do it your way.

Yes, this is a takeoff from Frank Sinatra's song, where he did it his way and got away with it. You're building a company from your vision and a passion, and lots of people are going to tell you that you have this or that wrong, and that it just won't work.

The truth is that very, very few early business plans survive in a form completely recognizable when looking back a few years. But even with massive changes, the vision and passion usually don't diminish in the process of morphing a business plan into a profitable business.

Investors will invariably try to tell you that they know much more about the "how to" than you do, and that you should listen to them. And because you need their money, the temptation is to listen a bit too well, and take all of the advice thrown at you during your presentations and during due diligence and finally from the vantage point of a board seat. A good entrepreneur-turned-CEO listens, takes it all in, responds with reason, and stands up for what s/he believes for the parts that matter most. It is good to listen. And it is better to assimilate the best suggestions into your cake as you bake it.

But there is a limit, a point where your gut is more important than your ear. If you reach that point with suggestions from these people trying to help, think carefully about how to respond, whether with facts, instinct or support from others. Make your case for staying the course. Remember the same passion you demonstrated when you first attracted these well-meaning helpers. And push back. Some investors may drop out if you are in the pre-funding stage. But they are not the ones whose support you would later want. Some board members may show dismay. But most often, a good case made with passion wins the day and unites the group to move forward.

I was chairman of an excellent company where I had led the deal, attracting angel investors through several rounds as the company grew to a breakeven with over four million dollars of gross revenues. We then sought and received a venture investment from a top tier Silicon Valley VC firm, whose partner came onto the board. After several months on the board, he spoke up. "I don't like the niche we're in. It will never grow enough to make this a valuable company. Forget this niche and turn the battleship. Let's go after the Fortune 50." "But that's walking away from an industry where we are #2, growing nicely and already becoming profitable," the CEO responded.

"Don't worry. We'll be there in six months when you run out of money with your new R&D focus", the VC board member replied. The rest of the board, including myself, went along with this because, as I've stated often, *the last money in has the first say. (See more on page 54.)*

Can you guess the end to the story? Six months later, the company ran out of cash, as planned, when ceasing to focus on the original niche. And the VC firm's partners voted not to fund the restarted venture. A good company, in a fine industry, ended up being dismantled just to repay the bank loan. No investors received anything. And the rest of us just shook our collective heads. No one stood up to the VC board member, even though all of us heard but ignored our respective gut responses pushing back, as we remained silent.

It is years later, and the memory of that failure to push back remains fresh for me and surely for the rest of the former board members. As chairman, I should have pushed back. Certainly the CEO-founder had a duty to push back. Another VC from a smaller company should have pushed back. In retrospect, we were intimidated by the first tier VC, and half wanted to believe that he knew something we did not.

He did not. Now, with that lesson firmly behind, I often remind members of a board when in a situation where someone on the board pushes to change the plan that the vision of the founder ignited us to bring us together. If we believe we have a better idea, we should convince the founder and the rest of the board that we have strong beliefs that dispute the current plan. But we should not be so loud as to drown out those other voices - you know - the ones from the gut and that of the founder's dream.

Fail fast!

Professional investors want to live by this rule. With the first round of funding, there should be milestones to be achieved. If they are not achieved within the expected time, the reasons must be analyzed and acted upon to avoid loss of capital beyond plan or expectation.

And if the vision of the entrepreneur is flawed, or the product impossible to create within cost and time expectations, or the demand impossible to quantify, or revenues never close to plan, then it is time to rethink the plan and product. An excellent management team is perhaps the greatest asset for any company because it is just this team that has historically been able to make a drastic alteration of the plan, ultimately making a failing vision into a wildly successful one.

But if neither great management nor the entrepreneur's vision for the product shows real signs of success in the market, it is the hope of professional investors that the company fails fast, reducing further expenditures of remaining capital and protecting the assets purchased with the original investment.

My favorite story of a fast failure was of a technology incubator started in the year 2000 with optimistic money from a number of angel investments, including mine. Within a month after the tech crash, the founder of the incubator (who remains a close friend) decided that it made no sense to incubate companies that were not likely to receive new investments soon following incubation in the winter-of-cash that followed the tech crash. He volunteered to close the incubator and returned 96% of our investments to all of the angel investors. (That return proved to be the best investment return any of us saw in the several years that followed.)

Half of all professionally managed venture capital or angel investments fail. There should be no shame to the entrepreneur in admitting such a failure. Some angel and VC investors will give special credit to those entrepreneurs who have experienced failures when investing in their next effort. The lessons learned are difficult to teach and are great assets in the next effort.

Your Mobile Digital Native Starter Kit.

An amazing transformation is taking place in the work place. As the new generation of *digital natives* enters the work force, management is being pressed to open their networks and their thinking to allow social networking inside the firewall, workers who are more productive and comfortable anywhere but in a cubicle, and management of a virtual workforce. Mobile workers are quickly overtaking the fixed desk worker in developed countries, quickly catching up with Japan, where this has been the majority behavior for several years.

You already know the freedom gained by the use of wireless devices - offices that follow you instead of tie you down, and call attention to the power of virtual workers. Here is a practical list of empowerment tools for you as entrepreneur out to conquer the world with your vision and energy. After all, even the woodsman or guitarist starts with his favorite axe.

To enable these new nomadic workers to be productive, developers have created hundreds of thousands of applications for the iPhone, iPad, Android devices, and for Facebook users.

This brings us to my personal list of the ten most important – essential – things we digital natives need to un-tether from our cubicles and desks and be at least as productive at home or anywhere. You may have a different list, but here is mine…

1.   **A great smartphone.** More than half of the people on the planet now have cell phones, and the smartphone with Internet and enterprise system access is the fastest growing segment, long since more than half of all phones sold.   Most any of these models work well for a digital native who can then state with passion, *"I have an office in my pocket!"*

2.   **Collaboration tools**: GoToMeeting, WebEx, FreeConference.com, Skype, Google Docs, Vokle, and others: Some are now available on the

smartphone as well as desktop and even built into some newer HD-TV's. Skype provides the infrastructure for cost-free video and audio conferencing and long distance dialing with sound quality often exceeding that of normal communication channels.

3. **Internet access via cellular networks:** If the theme is "un-tethering" from a fixed broadband land line, then a great wireless device is a must. Variations on the theme include cards that broadcast WIFI signals to a small area, built-in to netbooks and tablets and more.

4. **Wireless desk phone system:** I discovered the power of this one recently when installing a new wireless attachment for my desktop phone system, allowing me to walk up to 300 feet from my desk with a belt-clipped remote and up to 30 feet from that remote with the included Bluetooth earpiece. The system seamlessly receives calls from my desk phone, my cell phone and my desktop Skype with equal ease as I roam the office environment.

5. **A follow-me account**: Although many digital natives have cut the cord literally and done away with landlines, the rest of us would like to have up to five phones ring simultaneously, and roll over to a single voicemail if we do not answer any of them in a set time. *Vonage and Google Voice* are services providing this great feature at no additional cost for the freedom it provides.

6. **A compact all-in-one:** When we are at home with our limited space and resources, a great all-in-one printer, scanner, and fax is a necessity. I prefer a black and white laser unit with a small footprint for low cost pages and quiet operation, delivering quiet inexpensive pages when needed, and color scanning to the computer.

7. **A netbook or tablet:** I no longer carry a large notebook, but rather a mini-note (or netbook or tablet such as the iPad or an Android tablet). It is all in the name of longer battery life, less space and less weight. The arrival of the iPad and competing devices add both complexity and

simplicity at the same time. I will carry both my netbook and an iPad wherever I travel, combining the book reader and application-friendly iPad with the workhorse netbook for office work and presentations.

8.   A portable scanner and/or portable printer: If you haven't seen or worked with a pencil-thin portable scanner, you haven't experienced the ability to digitize at will anything you run across in your travels. Only ½ inch round by 9 inches long, you will forget you have this in your bag or pocket until you need an instant copy of a news article, a document or an invoice. And sometimes, we just have to give in to the fact that the paperless office is not going to be a reality soon, especially when we are away from our desks for more than a few days

9.   The small resource bag: All of us need an extra USB memory stick, chargers, cables and even a second battery. Some of us add a wireless remote for presentations, a laser pointer and a few small screwdrivers.

10.   The wild card: Here is your chance to add that tool relevant to your needs. I would split the wild card into two items if I could: a docking station with keyboard and monitor ... and a portable projector, which is not for everyone, but for most of us who make presentations on the road and sometimes on the spot. There is a new generation of tiny projectors in the market to allow the mobile worker to share without notice. For full room size presentations, I carry a slim XGA projector, only 1.7" high and 8x10" in size, weighing 4 pounds and able to fill a large meeting room with a beautiful picture. For smaller projections, there are devices small enough to be carried in your pocket. And new cell phones with digital projectors are now available for smaller presentations.

You'll have your own "must have" list. Whatever our disagreement, let's celebrate our personal digital empowerment and collective un-tethering from a fixed business desk.

What about previous company non-competes?

Entrepreneurs tend to remain in the business arena they came from. Some are alumni from companies that would be a competitor to the enterprise being created or joined. And some are former selling shareholders of just those businesses. What is the rule about those pesky non-compete agreements signed upon discharge or sale of the previous company?

The good news is that if you were not a significant (usually 5% or more) selling shareholder of a previous company, many states specifically exempt non-compete agreements signed between companies and their employees or minority shareholders. In that case, you must worry only about information and trade secrets taken from the previous company which are both certainly subject to protection by almost all laws and courts.

So, to everyone: do not take customer lists, design documents or any document considered a trade secret from any previous employer or previous consulting customer. Yes, some companies were sloppy and did not have you sign a confidentiality agreement, but that procedural slip does not protect you from their legal wrath. Further, there is no expiration on these documents. You cannot complain that the document or information in question is more than five years or two employers old.

Set a realistic goal. When reached, set another.

There's a big difference between your vision for your company, your mission and your goal. Your vision tells the world what you want to be as you contemplate in advance how you will change the world for the better. Your mission merely states who you are and what you do. It is used to limit and sift your opportunities to keep you from using resources for projects outside of your core, your mission.

But your goal is a tangible aiming point, one that should be achievable within several years if you accomplish your progressive steps planned between now and then. You can express it in terms of money, market share, influence or other measure that reflects success. An example: "To be at a $25 million run rate by the end of our fifth year in business." That is measurable and from this you'll be able to look backward to develop a set of steps (strategies) to achieve that goal.

Once achieved, a goal is meant to be overwritten with a newer one, set to even higher standards. If achieved early, celebrate and set another goal earlier than planned.

The good thing about a goal is that it is measurable, and progress toward it can be measured as well. Unlike a mission or even a vision, neither of which may be measured, there is a satisfaction in each step toward achievement. Better yet, your employees and investors will appreciate constant attention to the goal and reports of progress toward it. A goal serves as a rallying point for all associated with your vision.

Make the goal realistic, achievable and public. You'll find others buying into the objective and even creating better ways to achieve it because they are invested in the dream and the measure of that dream – the mutual goal.

Map your goal and use your map.

It's time to speak of some sort of business plan. As a professional investor in early stage companies, I have long discounted long, detailed business plans in favor of a concise "executive summary" followed by a believable spreadsheet-based financial forecast projecting three to five years into the future.

Yes, everything does change between drafting that plan and its successful execution. But flying without a map of some kind seems just plain too risky.

I recently joined the board of a company that was growing slowly, running beyond breakeven, but had not approved a plan for the current year, let alone attempted to develop one for the next. So the CEO had one of his own that he did not share, while the CFO had one for internal use that was never shown to the CEO or to the Board. No wonder the Board members wanted to dig in and find who was communicating with whom, and who was in charge of the map to the goal. By the way, there was no goal understood by all or agreed to by anyone. How do you compensate executives and all levels for successful accomplishments if there are no established steps toward the goal? And how do you measure a person's contribution to an unnamed goal?

So if you have not, create a concise map for your enterprise. Start with a reasonable goal, usually expressed as a revenue number some number of years in the near future. Assess your current resources and attempt to calculate the resources needed to accomplish the goal. Do you need to raise money, focus spending upon only core projects that advance the company toward the goal, or bring in new management talent to make it happen? Write these steps down in any form for now. We'll explore a more organized approach in the next insights.

Strong strategies + tactics support your goal.

Now we're getting organized. There are many ways to express the roadmap for your enterprise. One of the most popular was used by the U.S. Army late in World War II, and adopted by a number of high profile businesses such as Texas Instruments after the War. The structure combined the listing of the goal with a series of strategies and then tactics, each designed to support each other, each measurable and made public throughout the organization. The technique, "OST" (objective, strategies and tactics), is a very good way to organize your effort to find guideposts and then develop metrics to measure progress.

What is a strategy? It is a medium range process involving senior management and departmental management as well, directing resources in ways that, as accomplished, lead the company toward the goal. A typical small to medium, business finds five sweeping strategies for the current year, many cross-departmental, and some carried over from the previous year's plan and even from years before that. Here are some example strategies from some of my companies over the recent years.

- Expand into at least three new continents through new distribution channels.

- Penetrate the Fortune 500 with at least five active accounts within two years.

- Create a hosted "software as a service" or "on demand" addition to our product line by end of (next) year.

Note that these are expansive "junior" goals that, if achieved, would certainly move the company forward toward a larger financial goal. Yet each is measurable if achieved. In fact, the degree of progress toward achievement can also be achieved, such as "We did establish and do business with two of the five Fortune 50 accounts this year."

Measurement is the key to success. Even at the strategic level. Next we'll look at the last major step in creating an OST plan for an entire organization.

Five strategies + five tactics = one goal

In past insights, we explored the need for a tangible goal and strategies that are measurable as steps toward achievement of the goal. This insight calls to account tactics to accompany each strategy, and even suggests a number for each.

Tactics support strategies and allow your individual managers and departments to contribute to strategies in measurable ways that are more short term and procedural than are the strategies they support. Tactics change frequently as achieved and may be updated or replaced during a year when achieved, unlike strategies which often span a number of years.

Five tactics to support each strategy seem a fair, even if arbitrary number. Tactics direct each department in very specific ways. Here are several examples of tactics from my recent experience with companies where I serve as board member.

Strategy Three: Expand into at least three new continents through new distribution channels.

1. Sign one distributor by June of this year in each of three major geographic areas. EMEA, Asia, Latin America. Each distributor to be capable of generating $1 million in business by year two.

2. Assign development manager to localize design and oversee needed enhancements to product and support materials for each new territory.

3. Train and transfer technology to each new distributor within 90 days of signing.

4. Assign one corporate employee to support sales and installation efforts by all distributors.

5. Seed demand in each new territory with at least two corporate marketing events in partnership with each distributor.

Note that each of these tactics directly support the strategy, are measurable and assumed to be achievable, bought into by each department effected by the tactic. Note that the strategy calls for cooperation between business development, sales, marketing, product development, installation and support. This is a great way to unify departments that once may have competed for resources toward individual ends, now pointed toward a common goal supported by all levels of management up to the CEO.

In planning, the matrix, "5x5=1" is a good memory tool for management to keep from overreaching with too many strategies and too many tactics. But it is not written in stone. And development of these important elements of the plan should be made using all the resources available, from your board of directors to your senior management to departmental management. Getting all to buy into each step may not be easy, but when accomplished, is a powerful and invigorating opportunity to celebrate, then to get to work as a functional unit of the whole.

Your budget and forecast light your goal.

Let's spend a few moments defining a sometimes confusing set of terms. A budget should be created each year as a result of a series of negotiations between departmental managers and their superiors through to the CEO, all in support of the next year's tactics previously agreed upon (which in turn support the longer term strategies leading to the next goal beyond).

So a budget sets the limits upon spending for the next year that are negotiated between the players. An important part of the budget is the expected revenue for the coming year, a critical factor in setting hiring and resource expectations for the year. During the year, if the forecast revenues fall short or are greatly exceeded, it is fair to revise the budget and rethink hiring and resources. Otherwise, it is the expectation of the board of directors of a company that each year's budget be approved in advance and adhered to as long as revenue goals are met.

Note that I used the term "forecast" for revenues for the next year. The term is also used when projecting revenues for succeeding years. The term "forecast" is a bit confusing, because it is also used by some as a measure of expected revenue and expenses to the end of the current year, found by taking actual performance year-to-date and adding best estimates of remaining revenues and expenses for the rest of the year to obtain an expected or "forecast" outcome at yearend. Both uses of the term are common. Just be sure all who participate understand which use of the word is the current one.

The real point here is to create a financial plan to support the strategic plan, marrying them in harmony one with another. Many entrepreneurs are impatient by nature, not the best of detailed planners. Yet, with the assistance of those in support such as the CFO, everyone in management must be aligned in a single direction, reviewed and updated annually as accomplishments, the marketplace, and even the competitive landscape change.

Use metrics and dashboard. Act upon variances.

Have you ever driven a car that had no speedometer? I had that thrill when a student at the Richard Petty Stockcar School of Driving recently at a motor speedway in California. With a wide track, angled aggressively at the curves, and being told to hug the wall on the straightaways, there was little reference available to a novice driver as to speed. I followed my instructor's car closely, but still could not tell anything about my speed, so that I could either compensate for lags behind the leader or to test my comfort zone at various points that matched the expectation of my instructor and my own increasing capabilities as a driver. Upon conclusion of eight laps of this, after pulling into the alley and climbing through the window on the driver side (there are no doors in these cars), I was handed a sheet with my timings for each of the eight laps. Only then, after when the information might have been useful, could I see how well I did.

That's how you would feel if you ran your company without a dashboard containing relevant metrics that drive your company. If you cannot relate to this, then you probably have been driving without a speedometer from the start and need to pay particular attention.

Metrics should be created by you and your managers to measure near real time progress for your enterprise. A number of these deemed critical to you and your managers should be combined into a single page on your desktop screen or in printed form and available or circulated as often as daily. These measures of progress must be fresh and meaningful. Yesterday's sales and returns compared to same day last week and last year for retail businesses; Units produced and units shipped compared to plan and same period last month for manufacturers; Yesterday's overtime hours by department; Ratio of hours worked to units produced; Backorders unshipped; Customer service calls in cue or unresolved.

You can think of numerous critical measures for your business that must not be ignored, but often are neglected by senior management. It is not bad to manage by walking around, a term that became popular as a result of another of the many business advice books of the '90's. But that method, although good for employee morale, is imprecise as a tool of measurement and should be relegated to a supporting role. Financial information for last month compared to plan and same month last year is certainly relevant, but not part of a dashboard, since there is nothing you can do to fix a problem when numbers are as old as a week, let alone the typical several weeks required to prepare financial statements for review.

Finally, what good is the information contained in a great dashboard if you ignore it? Show that you value the information by acting immediately upon variances, even if only to question the numbers. Everyone down the line will become aware of your attention to their work, your interest in the outcomes and care for their success. And you will drive revenue and better control costs and the customer experience with quick reaction to the variances within critical metrics that best describe your immediate situation.

So we have come to the arbitrary end of business state one – ignition. You have planned for, created and organized a fine business with minimum friction from un-oiled parts. You've hired the best and found ways to measure their workflow that are meaningful to all. Perhaps you did all this with your own capital from savings or from credit card debt. But at some point the growth of your enterprise will be throttled by the need for capital. And you will probably consider external sources for that capital early in the fundraising process. Stage two of *Berkonomics* is set to quickly explore the sources and responsibilities that come from such capital-raising.

Learn the science - practice the art of negotiation.

From the time we learn to manipulate our parents from the crib to the present day, we learn to negotiate to obtain our wants and needs. As we grow, we negotiate constantly with our parents, then with our peers. As we enter the business world, we negotiate with our bosses and our subordinates. We negotiate with our suppliers, customers, investors, and even our auditors. At home, we certainly negotiate with our spouses or significant others.

If we are constantly negotiating to obtain an advantage or just a win-win attempt at parity, we should make an effort to learn and then practice the art of negotiation (although I prefer to think of it as a science then delivered in its final form as art.)

Because I believe that negotiation is so important to our success in the business and in the social world, I re-read my favorite book on the subject again every couple of years, just to keep myself aware and sharp using the tools and techniques so important to a successful negotiation. The book, *You Can Negotiate Anything*, by Herb Cohn was first published in 1980 and is available today as the best and easiest to read of all the books on the subject. I implore you to read this book and internalize the three crucial variables, the many styles of negotiation, and the fourteen powers you can call upon or recognize when used by others in a negotiation.

Over the years, I have been delegated by a number of entrepreneurs and boards to negotiate critical agreements, sometimes to sell the company or merge it with another. I was selected because I did not have an emotional stake in the outcome as did the entrepreneur, or the continuing relationship with a buyer as would others in management who might remain after the sale. With that freedom, I was able to use the tools of negotiation to achieve a result better than if I worried each moment about disrupting the deal when making each move and countermove. There is a lesson there, one the same Herb Cohn quoted in a later book, in which he entreated his readers to negotiate with care, but *"not that much care"* as to lose perspective.

I recall one such instance, when delegated to be the lead in negotiating a sale of a company on whose board I sat, I asked the entrepreneur to name his expected price in an ideal sale, which he did immediately as if he'd been thinking of this for some time. Surprising him and the rest of the board, I asked him to go home and not to attend the negotiation session set for that evening at a local hotel, promising to call him immediately with the outcome. I am sure he worried over losing control of his most important business negotiation ever, but he did cede the task to me (and another board member).

Doing my homework ahead of time, using one of Herb Cohn's principles (*please* read the book), at the start of the negotiation I placed a paper in front of the negotiator representing the intended buyer, showing how our company would be accretive to their public company valuation, properly valuing our purchase at three times the ideal amount as stated by our entrepreneur-CEO. The buyer looked over the numbers for a few minutes, recognizing the accuracy of my statement from his due diligence and knowledge of his own financials. In a sincere response so transparent as to be an obvious truth, he stated, "Oh, but I only have authority from the Board to offer two-thirds of that" which of course was twice our entrepreneur's the asking price.

After forty-five minutes of further negotiation, we walked from the room with an agreement to sell the company for cash at twice the asking price. And as the entrepreneur still tells the story, we two board members walk on water for having delivered such great results. In fact, we had done our homework, presented a logical case, and created a win-win by leaving enough value for the buyer to add to its market capitalization as well as doubling our sales price.

Since we negotiate daily for things large and small, wouldn't it be high on your list to learn to use the tools and be aware of the elements of a great negotiation?

Good hearts finish first.

People argue over whether an entrepreneur with a sense of fairness, a desire for collegiality, a want to share the profits can succeed in the long run within a business world full of lions and tigers that eat timid entrepreneurs for lunch.

First, let's separate the "good heart" from the issue of whether an entrepreneur is driven to succeed. A sense of values that allows for sharing and fairness is not at odds with a 'type A' entrepreneur driven for success.

What is important is that stakeholders (people working for and with the entrepreneur) accept the entrepreneur for his or her good intentions, sense of fairness and willingness to listen.

I have had numerous experiences during my business career where business people I dealt with took advantage of the moment selfishly because they could, not because they should. I recall an executive who kept a large deposit but canceled a contract, refusing to negotiate, because the next payment due was a few days late. Or another who sued over a gray area issue, refusing to listen or negotiate. (He lost the suit and paid both sides' fees.)

And I have come to the conclusion that "good guys" (men and women) do finish first. There is no scientific proof, no metric to measure the full meaning of "good." and no special acknowledgement from any "good-watching" organization. Even without these, I am sure of this.

Surely the ruthless more often win in the short run. But early successes, built upon the broken backs of adversaries, are rarely followed by long- term wins for the tyrant or for the tyrant's company.

Be of good heart. You will enjoy your entrepreneurial or managerial ride much more, and your stakeholders will follow you through the flames as well as cheer your successes.

About the author...

Dave Berkus has a proven track record in operations, venture investing and corporate board service, both public and private. As an entrepreneur, he has formed, managed and sold successful businesses in the entertainment and software arenas. As a private equity investor, he has obtained healthy returns from liquidity events in over a dozen investments in early-stage ventures. As a corporate mentor and director, he was named *"Director of the Year"* for his directorship efforts with over 40 companies in the past decade.

Dave was the founder of **Computerized Lodging Systems Inc.,** *(CLS),* which he guided as founder and CEO for over a decade that included two consecutive years on the *Inc.500* list of America's fastest growing companies, expansion to six foreign subsidiaries and twenty-nine foreign distributors, while capturing 16% of the world market for his enterprise products. Known as a hospitality industry visionary with many "firsts" to his credit and for his accomplishments in advancing technology in the hospitality industry, in 1998 he was inducted into the **Hospitality (HFTP)** *"International Hall of Fame,"* one of only thirty so honored worldwide over the years.

He has made over 100 investments in early stage ventures, for which he has an IRR of 97%, which includes capital contributions to his two funds (**Berkus Technology Ventures, LLC** and **Kodiak Ventures, L.P.**, for which he is the managing partner). He is also Chairman Emeritus of the Tech Coast Angels, one of the largest angel networks in the United States.

In recognition for adding significant shareholder value for emerging technology companies over the past decade, he was named *"Director of the Year-Early Stage Businesses"* by the *Forum for Corporate Directors* of Orange County, California and *"Technology Leader of the Year"* by the Los Angeles County Board of Supervisors. Dave currently sits on ten corporate boards and four non-profit boards.

Dave is also a senior partner in the twenty year old consulting firm of *Hospitality Automation Consultants, LTD (HACL)*, and lends his considerable visionary and strategic talents to worldwide hospitality chains and groups. He is the partner responsible for business process reorganization, strategic planning, software development and wide-area network infrastructure, and enterprise management systems.

A graduate of Occidental College, Dave currently serves as a Trustee of the College. Aside from this book, he is author of fourteen other books, twelve in the **BERKONOMICS** series, *"Extending the Runway"* originally published by Aspatore Press (and now by the BERKUS Press), and co-author of *"Better than Money!"* All are books for emerging growth technology company executives. Dave serves as Board Member of the San Gabriel Valley Council of **Boy Scouts of America**, former Board Member of the **Forum for Corporate Directors**, and is Chairman of the Advisory Board of the technology arm of the **ABL Organization**, a networking organization of CEOs in high tech businesses.

He is often engaged as keynote speaker for events worldwide, speaking on trends in technology and of legal and practical issues of governance for emerging company corporate boards. He tells stories of entrepreneurs who have wildly succeeded or failed, deriving lessons from each for his audience. His TEDx talk, *"Smile at success; Laugh at failure,"* is available on YouTube as are other of segments of his keynotes. His televised *"Berkus Report"* segment of *Eye on Business*, can be found on Time Warner cable and other cable channels nationwide.

To contact Mr. Berkus for speaking engagements or workshops, email dberkus@berkus.com **, or phone (626)355-5375. Dave's books are available for purchase from the above website, or the same source from which this book was purchased.**

Subscribe to the free weekly email or blog, www.Berkonomics.com**, containing much of the information from Dave's books with lots of comments from readers with their own stories to tell.**

Follow Dave on Twitter (@daveberkus) and Facebook (Dave.Berkus).

Other books by Dave Berkus available directly from *www.berkus.com* or from your favorite bookseller or online store:

EXTENDING THE RUNWAY
Aspatore Press / Thompson West Publications

The five tools board members and executives can use to help their companies succeed.   How boards and CEOs should relate to each other for growing the enterprise. Fifty-eight critical questions boards and management should consider in order to assure their mutual alignment.

BASIC BERKONOMICS
Hard cover, soft cover and eBook editions

Volume one of this series. Over one hundred critical insights for entrepreneurs, CEOs and board members covering the life of the company from ignition through liquidity event.   Written with basic explanations for terms and methods, as well as insights into planning and measurement for success with small business startups.

BERKONOMICS
Hard cover, soft cover and eBook editions

Volume two of this series. One hundred and one critical insights for entrepreneurs, CEOs and board members covering the life of the company from ignition through liquidity event.   Dave tells over fifty stories to illustrate his insights, culled from his experience as entrepreneur and service on over forty corporate and ten non-profit boards.

BERKONOMICS WORKBOOK

Companion to BERKONOMICS, this very personal journal contains 101 exercises for the CEO or manager that make each of the insights contained in BERKONOMICS come to life in the form of provocative and actionable questions to be answered right on the pages of the workbook. Once completed, this workbook becomes the manager's personal blueprint for business growth.

ADVANCED BERKONOMICS

Hard cover, soft cover and eBook editions

Volume two of this series. One hundred and one critical insights for entrepreneurs, CEOs and board members covering the life of the company from ignition through liquidity event.   More advanced insights into planning and measurement for success with small business startups.

SMALL BUSINESS SUCCESS SERIES
A Series of eight short and inexpensive books or eBooks

Take all the great material in the BERKONOMICS series and slice it by subject, and you'll have these eight inexpensive, short books about issues that you and your management team needs to focus upon today. Ideal for giving to your entire management group for group discussions and business planning sessions.

BOOKS and eBOOKS IN THIS SERIES:

1. Starting up!
2. Raising Money
3. Positioning for Success
4. Managing your Workforce

5. Protecting your Business
6. Growing your Business
7. Building Great Boards
8. Cashing Out!

www.ingramcontent.com/pod-product-compliance
Lightning Source LLC
Chambersburg PA
CBHW022123170526
45157CB00004B/1732